Eating Out in Santa Fe

ALL the Best Restaurants, Cafes, Markets, Bakeries & Street-Eats

Judith Wolf

Photography by Guy Cross

Bridgeline Books

FIRST EDITION

Designed and produced by Peggy Mackenzie, Sonoma, CA

Photo on page 25 copyright © Scott Christopher
Photo on page 37 by Matt Gray, copyright © THE magazine
Photo on page 81 copyright © Jackie Mathey
All other photographs copyright © Guy Cross

Library of Congress Cataloging-in-Publication Data

Wolf, Judith
    Eating out in Santa Fe: all the best restaurants, cafes, markets, bakeries, and street-eats/ Judith Wolf; photography by Guy Cross. — 1st ed.
    p.   cm
    Includes index.
    ISBN 1-888843-37-3 (trade paper)
    1. Restaurants—New Mexico—Santa Fe—Directories. 2. Cookery—New Mexico—Santa Fe. 3. Santa Fe (N.M.)—Description and travel.
I. Title.
TX907.3.N62S268   1997
647.95789'56—dc21   97-5732
                                                                                    CIP

97 98 99 100   10 9 8 7 6 5 4 3 2

This edition is printed on recycled paper.

To Buddy

ACKNOWLEDGEMENTS

I particularly thank my husband, Guy Cross, whom I married in the midst of writing this book. He gave me the courage and support to do it, and put up with complaints of tired eyes, sore neck, headaches, and all kinds of hysteria and nonsense.

Thanks to my daughter, Shawn Lee Wharton, and son-in-law, Jamie Meade, who, among other things too numerous to mention here, gave me an indispensable culinary resource book for Christmas that I use everyday.

Thanks to Bunny Conlon, who introduced me to New Mexican food and ate a lot of chile with me over the years, to Lucille Garfield who has such *joie de vivre* that she always made our eating experiences fun and adventurous, and Genevieve and Randolph Laub for contributing great style and extensive knowledge of wines every time we ate out together.

Special thanks to Rebecca Paxton and Lee Myers for their unflagging support and belief in me.

And many thanks to writers and cooks who inspired me over the years and taught me the joy of food: Julia Child, M.F.K. Fisher, Pierre Franey, Sheila Lukins, Deborah Madison, Julee Rosso, Lindsey Shere, Jeff Smith, Jane and Michael Stern, Martha Stewart, and Alice Waters, to name just a few.

Thanks to my publisher, Shirley Christine, for believing in this book and to her hard-working staff for making it possible.

And much gratitude to the chefs, cooks, and restaurants of Santa Fe for supplying the reason, and to my many other friends who helped contribute assistance and support.

▲▲▲▲▲▲
CONTENTS

7	Acknowledgements
9	Contents
11	Keys to Ratings and Prices
12	Area Maps
15	Introduction
15	Service
16	Reservations
16	Waiting in Line
16	Fresh from the Farm
16	Fish - Fresh or Frozen
17	Oriental Cuisine
17	New Mexican Specialties
17	Enchiladas
18	Chiles
19	Green Chile Stew
19	Tortillas
19	Margaritas
20	Mezcal
21	Southwestern Cuisine
21	Vegetarians
21	Cigar-Friendly
22	Art Influence
	Best Restaurants - In District Locations
23	Plaza and Downtown Area
71	Old Santa Fe Trail
78	Canyon Road and Area
86	South Guadalupe Street/Sanbusco Center
100	North Guadalupe Street Area
113	St. Francis Drive Area
117	Second Street
118	Cerrillos Road
126	Cordova Road
131	St. Michael's Drive
135	Rodeo Road
136	Tesuque
139	Chimayó
142	North of Santa Fe
144	South of Santa Fe

151   Best Bakeries
153   Best Farm
154   Best Food Event
155   Best Markets and Take-outs
162   Best Wine/Liquor Shops

Best Signature Dish Recipes:
24   Grilled Corn Tortilla Soup
with Gingered Pork Potstickers
(The Anasazi Restaurant)

30   Pan-Seared Atlantic Salmon
with Horseradish Sauce *(Cafe Escalera)*

35   Pollo Pibil with Saffron Rice & Fire-Roasted
Balsamic-Marinated Vegetables *(Cafe Pasqual's)*

39   Chipotle Shrimp with Corn Cakes and Pico de
Gallo Salsa *(Coyote Cafe)*

51   Polenta con Funghi al' Ungherese *(Julian's)*

64   Coriander Crusted Ahi Tuna
with Shaved Fennel Salad & Chile-Cilantro
Vinaigrette *(Santacafé)*

76   Chicken Hash Grits Ring *(The Pink Adobe)*

87   Crispy Polenta with Gargonzola Sauce *(Andiamo!)*

112   Vegetarian Grapeleaves *(Whistling Moon Cafe)*

Index:
165   District Locations
166   Types of Cuisine
168   Bakeries/Markets/Shops

KEY TO RATINGS

✪ ✪ ✪ Great food. Chef's signature dishes combined with a pleasant, often more formal, atmosphere and reliable service. One of Santa Fe's best.

✪ ✪ Very good food, chef on premises. Worth going out of your way for. Service can be inconsistent.

✪ Good food. Place often filled with happy, satisfied locals. There may be one or two outstanding items on the menu—read review first.

[Historical] A special, unique place, possibly a local legend and/or of historical interest. A must do. Ambience may be worth the special trip or a particular food item could be outstanding. Read review first.

KEY TO PRICES

Prices reflect one main lunch or dinner entree. (If a restaurant serves dinner and lunch, then the dinner entree is reflected.) Alcohol is not included in these prices.

Budget: $2 to $6

Inexpensive: $6 to $12

Moderate: $12 to $16

**Expensive/
Very Expensive:** $16 and up

Since a lot of Santa Fe restaurants feature seasonal menus with daily and/or weekly menu changes, some of the dishes mentioned may not always be available. The restaurant business is also constantly in flux; chefs may leave or move to other locations, restaurants may close or new ones may open, and addresses and price structures can change.

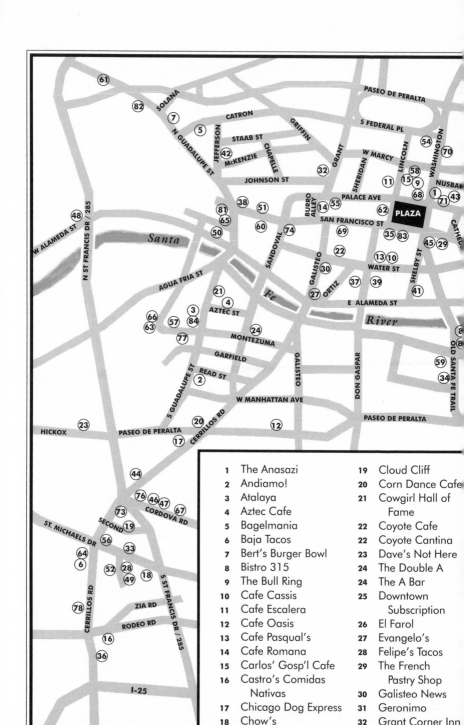

1	The Anasazi	19	Cloud Cliff
2	Andiamo!	20	Corn Dance Cafe
3	Atalaya	21	Cowgirl Hall of
4	Aztec Cafe		Fame
5	Bagelmania	22	Coyote Cafe
6	Baja Tacos	22	Coyote Cantina
7	Bert's Burger Bowl	23	Dave's Not Here
8	Bistro 315	24	The Double A
9	The Bull Ring	24	The A Bar
10	Cafe Cassis	25	Downtown
11	Cafe Escalera		Subscription
12	Cafe Oasis	26	El Farol
13	Cafe Pasqual's	27	Evangelo's
14	Cafe Romana	28	Felipe's Tacos
15	Carlos' Gosp'l Cafe	29	The French
16	Castro's Comidas		Pastry Shop
	Nativas	30	Galisteo News
17	Chicago Dog Express	31	Geronimo
18	Chow's	32	Grant Corner Inn

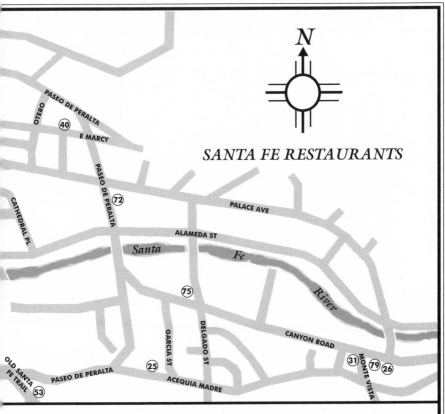

SANTA FE RESTAURANTS

33	Green Onion Sports Pub	**50**	Noon Whistle	**68**	Roque's Carnitas	
34	Guadalupe Cafe	**51**	The Old House	**69**	San Francisco St. Bar & Grill	
35	Haagen-Daz	**52**	Old Mexico Grill	**70**	Santacafé	
36	Horseman's Haven	**53**	Old Santa Fe Trail Bookstore & Bistro	**71**	The Shed	
37	Hotel St. Francis	**54**	Osteria	**72**	The Staab House	
38	Il Vicino	**55**	The Palace	**73**	Tecolote Cafe	
39	India Palace	**56**	The Pantry	**74**	Tia Sophia's	
40	Josie's	**57**	Pásale Bakery	**75**	Tibet Cafe	
41	Julian's	**58**	Paul's	**76**	Tiny's	
42	La Bell's	**59**	The Pink Adobe	**77**	Tomasita's	
43	La Casa Sena	**60**	Piñon Grill	**78**	Tortilla Flats	
44	La Choza	**61**	Pizza, Etc.	**79**	Trixie's	
45	La Plazuela	**62**	Plaza Restaurant	**80**	Upper Crust Pizza	
46	Maria's Kitchen	**63**	Portare Via	**81**	Vanessie	
47	Marisco's	**64**	Posa's	**82**	Whistling Moon	
48	Masa Sushi	**65**	Poulet Patate	**83**	Woolworth's	
49	Mucho: The Gourmet Sandwich Shoppe	**66**	Pranzo	**84**	Zia Diner	
		67	Pyramid Cafe			

RESTAURANTS
NORTH & SOUTH OF SANTA FE

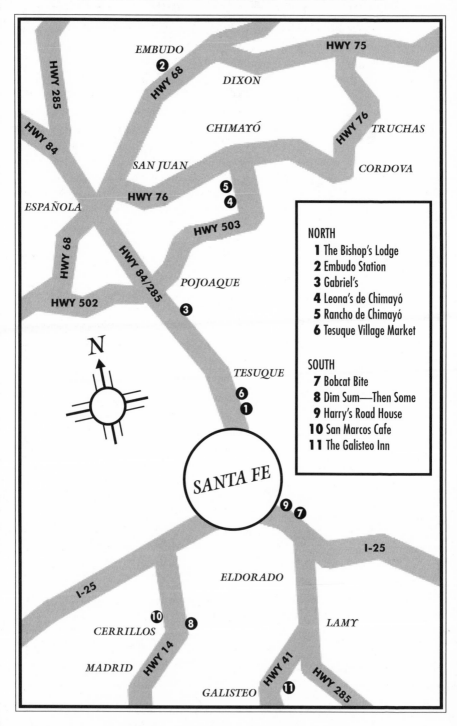

INTRODUCTION

*S*anta Fe is a city that is growing rapidly. Those who discovered this wild-west town way back in the 60s when all the roads were still dirt, and eating out meant a plate of flat-style enchiladas with "red or green" and an egg on top, would probably be surprised to now find a wide variety of eating experiences.

This is a city known for its cultural melting-cooking pot: Native Americans, Hispanics, Mexicans, Texans, and Californians have all contributed their special, distinct flavors and cuisines. The most recent immigrations from Texas, California, New York, and Boston, are bringing some of the best chefs and "foodie" intellectuals in America to Santa Fe. What this means, of course, is that Santa Fe is beginning to turn out some fine eating establishments (over 200 restaurants) and there is a general upgrade of food quality as a result of competition and superior local farm suppliers. Some upscale restaurants are already world-famous such as Santacafé and The Coyote Cafe.

Traditional New Mexican food is still, by far, the most popular—for locals and tourists—and can be found in abundance. Advice to the first-time visitor: New Mexicans are proud of their chiles. There are many different varieties of chiles with accompanying degrees of hotness and flavor complexities that go into almost every New Mexican dish. The chile sauces, red or green, can pack a wallop. So when ordering a dish with chiles, don't be shy about asking the waiter or waitress how hot the chile or the dish is—in fact, most restaurants will give you a small taste sample so you can decide for yourself.

Service

When I first visited Santa Fe in 1988, I thought that the restaurant service was the worst I had ever encountered. It seemed as if every server was "an emerging artist" and couldn't be bothered with such work as waiting tables. Unfortunately, this inexperience and attitude can still exist here. Advice: remain calm, make your order as clear as possible—speak up—don't whisper and make sure the wait person goes around the table in order. In other words, help out. I know it's an inconvenience but you'll be happier with the results in the long run.

There also can be some snobby wait persons in Santa Fe, the-I-know-more-than-you-do-because-you're-just-a-tourist kind. Part of the problem with service here is that Santa Fe is still a dirt-road town at heart and it really wants to remain that way. Of course that's part of it's charm.

The best advice is to keep a *mañana* mentality, be congenial, don't try to rush, and enjoy what is. However, some of the finest and best restaurants in Santa Fe have impeccable service—well trained and professional wait persons that add a pleasurable dimension to your eating experience. Some of the most knowledge-able and helpful waitpersons I've encountered in Santa Fe have been at the least expensive restaurants.

Reservations

Eating out has replaced theatre, movies, television, and other stimulating distractions for entertainment. When tourist season hits Santa Fe from June to December, most locals give up the idea of going out to eat because of crowded conditions and will settle for socializing at home.

Although a restaurant may say that they're booked up for weeks—even months ahead, call anyway. People have a habit of not showing up for their reservations, so call the day you want to go and ask about getting in that evening for dinner. Or better, call in the early evening and see if the restaurant can squeeze you in. It's surprising how often a table turns up empty.

Some restaurants are now implementing a policy of asking the customer who makes the reservation to call two days in advance to confirm and to also confirm with a credit card. If the customer does not call back, then the reservations are cancelled. This policy insures that reservations are intact and can open up tables for more serious diners.

Waiting in line

There are a few places in Santa Fe where reservations are not accepted—for lunch or dinner. One example where the queue gets long and those waiting get hot—or cold—depending on the season—is at Cafe Pasqual's. Try to go at an off-time (although Pasqual's never seems to have one), wear appropriate clothing, dive through the line and get your name on the waiting list. Ask about how long the wait will be, then either stroll over to the water fountain across the street, relax, and enjoy the time-honored pastime of people-watching or pop into Dootlet's just across the street from Pasqual's, for some silly, fun shopping.

Fresh from the Farm

Most visitors to Santa Fe are not aware of Northern New Mexico's short growing season. Farm areas surrounding Santa Fe like Abiquiu, Chimayo and Truchas, have generated incredible farms that equal California's and perhaps can even out-do them. For example, the famous Elizabeth Berry organic farm supplies over forty of the best restaurants in Santa Fe. There are also organic herb farms, garlic farms, tomato farms, dairy farms, and egg farms. Natural meats and poultry are also available. The Farmer's Market at Sanbusco Center in Santa Fe—outside in summer and inside year round—displays the best of Northern New Mexico honeys, preserves, breads, melons, corn, apples, tomatoes, greens, and other garden-fresh produce.

Fish - Fresh or Frozen

Another detail affecting "fresh" that many visitors may not be aware of is that Santa Fe and surrounding areas are approximately 7000-feet-high in altitude and land-locked. No oceans here. Many restaurants serve those delicious New Mexican trout fresh from our wild streams and rivers. But no matter how fresh the waiter or waitress tells you the fish is, double-check to see if it's fresh-frozen, or flown in fresh. Latest information is that fish and shellfish are flown fresh into Santa Fe at least twice a week—sometimes daily—so ask your service person, the restaurant manager, or owner to get the real facts.

Oriental Cuisine

San Francisco, we are not. So don't even begin to expect the same excellence as you will find in that city. You'll notice that this book does not list many Asian-style eateries. It's hard to tell if our area will ever catch up to the quality one finds in larger cities like San Francisco and New York. But if this is your preference, I have recommended a few restaurants in this guide.

New Mexican Specialties

"I'll have the Christmas enchiladas with blue corn tortillas please, flat, not rolled. And an egg on top with a side of posole. Does that come with sopaipillas? My friend will have the bowl of green—no beans."

New Mexico Mexican food is very different from Baja Mexican, or Mexico City Mexican or Sonoran Mexican or Yucatan Mexican or Texas Mexican or Southern California Mexican or any Mexican food. Pork, lamb, red and green chiles, blue corn, squash, rice, and beans, are traditional ingredients that are uniquely combined to create New Mexican cuisine.

The dishes that are made out of these ingredients have rich, Spanish names: *Atole* (a thin gruel-like drink made with blue or yellow corn meal), *Carne Adovada* (pork marinated in red chile sauce and baked), *Calabacitas* (Summer Squash), *Chauquehue* (thick blue corn gruel), *Quelites* (wild spinach-like greens seasoned with onions, chile, corn, and served with pinto beans), *Natillas* (thin custard), *Panocha* (sprouted wheat pudding), *Bizcochitos* (Anise cookies), *Empañadas* (the New Mexican version of meat and fruit pies), *Sopaipillas* (puffy, flakey, deep-fried bits of dough resembling little hollow pillows when they're done) and *Suspiros* (meringue cookies). The sopaipilla is supposed to have originated in Albuquerque over 200 years ago. Taking the place of bread, it is a staple with every New Mexican meal.

One of the most unusual sweets in New Mexico is the *Sopa/Capirotada* or bread pudding. What makes this dessert so unusual is its "secret" ingredient—Longhorn or Cheddar cheese.

Enchiladas

Enchiladas are *de rigueur* in Santa Fe. The first time I ordered an enchilada in Santa Fe I couldn't figure out where the "enchilada" was on my plate. My native New Mexican friend, Bunny Conlon, explained to me that in New Mexico it is traditional to prepare them flat or stacked rather than rolled (the form I was familiar with). Bunny always orders her enchiladas the way many New Mexicans do, "Vegetarian, Christmas, with an egg on top."

Bunny also told me a story about why the enchilada was created and why it originated without using meat: "The enchilada was created for New Mexico Fridays, the meatless day in Roman Catholic countries. So in families across New Mexico it was always 'enchi's on Friday's.'" Now enchiladas have evolved to include meats, crustaceans, fish, and heaven knows. So what is a Christmas enchilada? One with red *and* green chile, that's what.

Chiles

For the most comprehensive description and identification of chiles used most often in New Mexico restaurants, I recommend getting one or more of the many chile books available, such as *The Great Chile Book* by celebrated chef and restaurant owner, Mark Miller. The New Mexico green chile is the basis for New Mexican cusine and is available fresh, dried, or frozen all year.

The annual harvest of chiles (still in the immature stage—green) occurs in New Mexico in late August and early September when huge, wire cylinder ovens are set up in grocery store parking lots for roasting. The air is filled with acrid smoke from the chiles and can burn your eyes if you find yourself downwind from the roasters. Many locals purchase a fifty-pound gunnysack full of roasted green chiles to take home, skin, and freeze for use all through the winter. Historically, the mature, red chiles are dried whole and stored for use all year round—and still are, in the form of bright red, hand-tied ristras (they are traditionally tied into long strands and wreaths) and are available for purchase all over the city, at countryside homes, and markets.

There is an on-going argument among New Mexicans about what area in the state produces the best chiles and resulting chile powders. Some claim that the Chimayo chile is the best—sweeter and smoother than any other. Then there are those that swear by Pasilla's "red" ground chile that is sold in small packages by the Pasilla family on the roadside between Española and Mendanales (near Abiquiu). Hatch-grown chiles are world-renowned claiming to have the meatiest and sweetest chiles. And the battle goes on.

Red chile sauces in New Mexico are traditionally prepared from dried, ground red chile, prepared with water, a white flour roux, garlic, oregano (optional), basil (optional), and salt. It simmers for 15 minutes and is served with all the savory dishes that you'll experience here. Green chile is prepared from roasted, peeled, and seeded green chiles. Some add only garlic and water and others thicken it with flour. Oregano and cumin can also show up in green chile sauce. Even though simple in preparation, every restaurant that makes its own chile exhibits a wide range of flavor, texture, and heat. Chile heat depends on many things: For example, time of harvest and weather conditions during growth can determine how hot a chile can get. (Scientific update: The potent capsaicin that gives some chiles their fiery hotness is known for its decongestant qualitites and not only makes you perspire on the outside but makes sinuses and lungs "sweat" as well. An added benefit is that capsaicin produces endorphins in the brain promoting a sense of well-being.) Just to be on the safe side, eat red or green chile dishes every day or at least once a week.

Green Chile Stew

Green Chile Stew has become a status symbol in Santa Fe New Mexican restaurants. Locals have their favorite places to get it, and the stew is served in many different ways. Roasted green chiles can be combined with a meat or chicken broth, pork, potatoes, garlic, onions, and even tomatoes. Beans can be added if you ask and vegetarian green chile stew is available at most places. New Mexico's famous "bowl of green" is attributed to have magical, medicinal qualities. Suffering from a bad cold or the flu? Immediately eat some green chile stew—the hotter the better. Sinuses will open up and a cure will be forthcoming.

Tortillas

The blue corn variety of tortilla reigns supreme in New Mexico. Blue-gray in color from the blue corn it is made from, this tortilla mostly appears in corn chips and in enchilada dishes. Flour tortillas are traditionally used with burritos and quesadillas—they're made larger and are perfect for wrapping around good things.

Corn tortillas, as ancient as the Sandia Mountians, are the most widely used tortillas in the world. If combined with beans, rice, and salsa, you get a complete, nutritionally-correct meal. Corn tortillas show up in baskets—triangularly-cut and deep-fried—as tortilla chips.

Some restaurants make their own tortilla chips. When you taste the real thing you'll hate to go back to packaged chips. Did you know a handmade corn tortilla has an inside and an outside? According to an article on El Paso/Juarez border food in *Saveur's* January/February, 1996 issue, Luz Juarado said that the corn tortilla's inside "...has a little membrane of dough that can be lifted up ... and the outside of the tortilla is tough and smooth, able to withstand rolling and direct heat."

Margaritas

The search for the perfect margarita is one of those little pleasures that keep tequila afficionados and plain folk occupied in a life-long treasure hunt that often finds gold at the end of the tequila rainbow. Many restaurants in Santa Fe claim the perfect margarita. But in the end, it's not a matter of personal taste but the tequila used to make it.

A "real" margarita must first contain what is called "real" tequila—a liquor made only in Mexico that originally was made in the town of Tequila, in the state of Jalisco. It must contain at least 51 percent of the juices extracted from the heart of the blue agave or maguey plant and is aged anywhere from eight months to seven years.

A number, referred to as a NORMA, is issued by the Mexican government to Mexican tequila distillers to maintain strict regulations that produce tequila. A bottle of this type of tequila must have the three letters N-O-M followed by four numbers on the label. The best news is that tequila has come into its own with the exportation of super and ultra premium selects that are oak-barrel aged (anejo) and can be sipped neat. One such tequila is so special that only 4000 bottles were exported in 1995 (N-O-M 2213). The world's most expensive tequila you can buy right now is *Reserva de la Familia,* from the Jose Cuervo distillery, priced at $150 for a 1.75 liter bottle. Good luck trying to find some.

A good margarita must also contain freshly squeezed lime or lemon juice, no sugar. Now the going gets a bit rough. Maria's Kitchen in Santa Fe uses only lemon juice—not the traditional lime juice like in Mexico. Maria's claim is that lemons provide a year-round superior flavor consistency that cannot be found with the smaller, American-produced limes. (Margarita expert, Anne Kalminson, notes that perhaps it's citrus economics or that the American lemon more closely resembles the Mexican lime, thus making it more authentic in flavor.)

Triple-sec is another required ingredient—a clear orange liqueur made from the skins of exotic orange peels which have been sun-dried, reconstituted with distilled water, fermented, and then triple-distilled. Always check the label on the bottle of Triple-sec as some use artificial flavorings—a bad move. Cointreau is a premium Triple-sec imported from France that is widely used in margaritas as well as Grand Marnier, another French import blend of Triple-sec and Cognac that's aged for a minimum of eighteen months. Surprisingly, ice plays an important role in the margarita because it dilutes the drink with just the right amount of water. Blended or frozen margaritas are popular but not authentic—they add too much water that dilutes the natural flavors.

The most spectacular margarita selection I've ever come across in New Mexico was at Maria's Kitchen in Santa Fe—over 50 margaritas on the menu. The margarita that caught my eye was the 24-Karat Gold Reserva at $24. They say it is the most elegant margarita in the world. Salut!

Mezcal

In actual fact, all tequilas are mezcal. Surprised? Me, too. The many misconceptions that Americans have about mezcal have been cleared up thanks to the years of research completed by my Taos friend and mezcal importer, Ron Cooper. The word mezcal comes from Mexcalmetl, from the prehispanic Nahuatl language, meaning agave, or more commonly known as maguey in Mexico.

The rare mezcals imported by Ron Cooper are produced by local *palenqueros* in tiny remote villages scattered throughout the state of Oaxaca, Mexico, and are made by a natural process that is over four-hundred-years-old. The two ingredients used to make this pure mezcal are water and the heart of the maguey (or agave) plant—nothing more except the loving care given by the villagers in making it. There is a reverence and obvious pride regarding mezcal's power and purity among the people of Oaxaca. They believe it is a magical liquid; and they use it for ceremonial, social, and medicinal purposes.

If you want to experience a smokey, true, deep and warm mezcal that is certainly pure and perhaps even spiritual, I highly recommend Mezcal Chichicapa, a recent import from Oaxaca via Cooper's company, Del Maguey Limited. To preserve quality, production of this label is limited to 3,200 bottles per year. New labels of his company's imported mezcal will be forthcoming in 1997. Currently Mezcal Chichicapa can be found at the best liquor stores and restaurants in Santa Fe.

Cooper says, "The way mezcal affect's one's palate and the way it warms the chest, throat, and mouth are quite different than any other alcohol ever tasted."

Southwestern Cuisine

This term has been over-used, abused, and misused. Southwestern is a cuisine that has been created through the integration of many different tastes and flavors: Mexican, Tex-Mex, Hispanic, Cajun, Creole, and Native American. Chiles are a major part of this cuisine, contributing to the gutsy flavors that so characterize this style of cooking. Audacious chefs here in Santa Fe have mastered these combinations of complex flavors that make up Southwestern dishes and use direct methods of preparation like grilling and roasting that preserve the bold flavors. Santa Feans are indeed fortunate to have several restaurants that serve these foods with excellence and authority.

Vegetarians

The good news is that most of Santa Fe's restaurants offer meatless dishes. Because of Santa Fe's population of upscale new age and health-responsible folks, witnessed by the success of health food supermarkets such as Alfalfa and Wild Oats, it's easy to come by some great vegan and ovo-lacto-vegetarian meals. These two markets have lots of delicious take-outs to keep even the most die-hard vegetarians exalted.

Dairy and meat products are not always excluded so vegans—vegetarians who do not eat meat or any animal-derivative foods such as butter, milk, eggs, and cheese—must be careful. Some traditional Mexican cooking omits these items and uses only corn, beans, rice, chiles, and fresh salsas—no dairy, no meat.

If you include dairy in your diet, then you'll be a happy, ovo-lacto-vegetarian camper at almost all New Mexican restaurants.

Cigar-Friendly

A somewhat puzzling phenomenon, cigar events and dinners are now being held in Santa Fe on a regular basis at different "cigar friendly" restaurants.

Since the first issue of *Cigar Afficionado* came out on the stands, it took the United States by storm. The publisher admitted that all who gave advice doomed the publication to extinction. But, hidden sub-cults of cigar smokers and big-gun advertisers have made this publication a magazine success story. Consequently, cigar smokers are coming out of the closet to enjoy their cigar pleasures openly at distinctive restaurants around the country. Santa Fe is no exception.

There are quite a few cigar friendly restaurants here and that usually means that cigars may be smoked in designated areas within the establishment. At cigar dinners, however, the entire restaurant is set aside for a special night where cigars, wines, and foods are paired for the diners' consummate enjoyment. Cigar friendly restaurants are noted in this guide.

Art Influence

Santa Fe is recognized as the third largest art market in America with 150 art galleries and a local artist population of over 8,000. Artists have been coming here since the turn of the century to take advantage of the special light and minimal landscapes. Contemporary, traditional, and folk art continues to be an integral part of Santa Fe's social and economic fiber. Patrons of the arts, notably Anne and John Marion, have helped to create a Georgia O'Keeffe Museum, and have contributed to the development of a photographic department at the College of Santa Fe. Nationally-known artists and art-related experts come here to lecture and organize exhibitions for museums and private art institutions. Indian Market, held the third weekend in August, continues to draw tens of thousands of collectors and tourists to view and buy the finest of contemporary Indian art. In July, Spanish Market offers art created by Hispanic artisans. Site Santa Fe, a contemporary, multi-cultural art event—privately sponsored—brings famed international and national artists to Santa Fe in conjunction with New Mexico artists and our own Musuem of Fine Arts to create one of the finest, ongoing art events.

Local artists and artisans continue to form the backbone of Santa Fe's art community throughout the year. Examples of their work are on display in hundreds of galleries and many restaurants in the city.

▲▲▲▲▲▲▲▲▲▲▲
PLAZA - DOWNTOWN

The Anasazi Restaurant

✪ ✪ ✪

113 Washington Avenue. 988-3030. Located inside the Inn of the Anasazi.

Chef John Bobrick

Breakfast:	7 A.M.-10:30 A.M. Mon.-Sat.
Lunch:	11:30 A.M.-2:30 P.M. Mon.-Sat.
Dinner:	5:30 P.M.-10 P.M. daily.
Sunday Brunch:	7 A.M.-2:30 P.M. Sun.
Bar menu:	11:30 A.M.-11 P.M.
Features:	Full Bar. Smoke-free dining room. Smoking permitted in bar. Free valet parking. Art.
Price:	Moderate-Expensive. Major credit cards.
Cuisine:	Southwestern/American. (Menus change seasonally.)

*I*f you're one of the lucky who can stay at the Inn of the Anasazi—the *only* Santa Fe hotel listed in *Conde Nast Traveler* magazine as one of the "Top 50" mainland U.S. resorts—you'll be pleased to know that their restaurant is going to take good care of you. If you aren't a blessed one, not to worry, this eating establishment is open to the public and has become one of the best restaurants in Santa Fe.

The doors into the Inn's lobby also lead into a foyer that becomes the restaurant's petite bar. The main dining room is low-lit, creating a pueblo-like environment for diners. Tables are comfortably spaced around the room allowing diners to take in the art and Southwest-pueblo-style architecture.

The chefs and staff have made this soft-spoken-about place into an award-winning, top-drawer restaurant without the slightest fuss or commotion. The Anasazi received a Silver Award from the American Academy of Restaurant Sciences, as well as the prestigious AAA Four Diamond and Four Star Awards. I know, awards sometimes don't cut the dijon, but the food that the Anasazi presents to its guests is quite remarkable. Breakfast alone is amazing: *Whole Wheat Quesadillas with Lamb Sausage, Poached Eggs and Black Bean Hollandaise; Green Chile Duck Hash with Lime, Sage, and Grilled Tortillas; Cranberry Hazelnut French Toast with Dried Blueberries and Maple Syrup.* Whew!

Grilled Corn Tortilla Soup with Gingered Pork Potstickers

Ingredients for the broth:

8-1/2 cups corn tortillas, cut in strips	
3	jalapeños, half with seed
2	yellow onions, sliced
10	cloves garlic
8	ounces Sacramento tomato juice
1	tablespoon tomato paste
2	tablespoons cumin
1	tablespoon coriander
1/2	gallon chicken stock
1/2	cup olive oil
	Salt and pepper to taste

Method:

In large stock pot, heat oil until smoking. Fry jalapeños, garlic, and tortillas until crispy. Add onions and saute 2 minutes. Deglaze with tomato juice and chicken stock. Boil 10 minutes. Add cumin and cilantro. Season to taste with salt and pepper. Puree in food processor until smooth. Place broth in bowl. Top with 1/2 cup of tortilla strips and two potstickers.

Ingredients for the potstickers:

1/2	pound ground pork
1	tablespoon ginger, minced
1	tablespoon garlic, minced
2	tablespoons soy sauce
1	tablespoon sesame oil
1	tablespoon chile flakes
1	bunch green onions, sliced
1	bunch parsley, sliced
1	bunch cilantro, chopped
3	eggs
1	package of wonton skins
	Salt and pepper to taste

Method:

Combine all ingredients except wonton skins. Season to taste. Place small amount of mixture in skins and form to shape. Steam in double boiler until wonton skins are tender.

Yield: 16 cups

Photo by Scott Christopher

Don't stop at breakfast. But first get in some serious Plaza shopping and walk off breakfast.

Now for lunch —it's hard to resist the *Achiote Charred Rare Tuna with Wasabi Aioli and Snow Pea Slaw* or the *Mesquite Grilled Buffalo Burger on White Cheddar Jalapeño Brioche with Seasoned Fries and Yellow Ketchup with Vermont White Cheddar Cheese* or the *Salmon Club Sandwich with Apple Smoked Bacon and Charred Onion Aioli.* And you thought that was a tough decision.

Wait until you see the dinner menu. (By the way, all menus change according to the seasons.) The menu is original, creative, and innovative combining a variety of chiles with organic meats and poultry, and fresh organic produce and fruits. The kitchen takes an ordinary tamale and behold—*Charred Onion and Chihua- hua Cheese Tamale with Blackened Tomatillo, Papaya, Bean Salsa, and Tropical Barbeque*—just one of many fabulous appetizers. For the main entree you can't go wrong with the already-famous *Dry Rubbed Organic Tenderloin of Beef with White Cheddar Mashed Potatoes and Mango-Red Chile Jelly,* or the *Local Organic Lamb Rack with Two Tomato Mint Jelly and Mustard Roasted New Potatoes.*

Vegetarians are not forgotten at this restaurant with dishes like *Grilled Vegetable and Green Rice Rellenos with Tamarind Orange Pesto, Salsa Fresca and Ibarra Chocolate.* There is always fresh seafood on the menu too: *Peanut and Coconut Grilled Prawns with Spring Arugula, Tropical Fruits, Mint and Soya Ginger Vinaigrette.*

If, by chance, you didn't get enough of this distinctive cooking, drop in anytime from 11 P.M. to 2 A.M. during the Opera season (July and August) and try a dessert and espresso in the Inn's cozy Library.

The Bull Ring

**150 Washington Avenue (Located in First Interstate Plaza.)
983-3328.**

Lunch:	11:30 A.M.-3 P.M. Mon.-Fri.
Dinner:	5 P.M.-10 P.M. daily.
Features:	Full bar. Smoking/nonsmoking.
	Cigar friendly in bar only. Patio.
Price:	Moderate/Expensive. Major credit cards.
Cuisine:	American

This restaurant has been in business since 1971 and previously was located on Old Santa Fe Trail, close to the state capital's government buildings. It developed a reputation for its politico atmosphere—government officials of all levels would come for lunch and dinner to cement high-stake deals—a fact that may have prompted you to pull on hip boots before entering.

But Harry Georgeades, who has been in charge of The Bull Ring for the last fifteen years, moved his restaurant to a new location in 1995. This can be a portentous omen for restaurants—they can survive or fail—depending on local clientle or pure luck. Harry says the place continues to be a popular watering hole for New Mexican politicians, and dinnertime brings them in, *en force*. Though the new location doesn't have the same gritty feel as it once had, the operative word here is still *meat*. So, boots, grit, and legislators aside, serious meat eaters may want to try one of the Bull Ring's Cadillac-sized steaks for an old-fashioned steakhouse experience along with obligatory ice cold martinis and baked potatoes with all the stuff that goes on top. Steaks here are extraordinary—vegetarians need not apply: "USDA Prime, corn-fed mid-western beef" it says on the menu and "Our steaks are served sizzling in butter, specify extra butter or none." Prime beef (specially raised and aged) is hard, if not impossible, to come by for home barbeques, so indulge. Everything's a la carte (butter and cream sauces proliferate) and the selections are numerous—further celebrating America's love affair with fat.

There are eight kinds of potatoes including baked (with butter, sour cream, bacon, cheese, and chives), cottage fries, mashed, shoestring, Lyonnaise, and unmemorable au gratins; there's classic creamed spinach or asparagus with hollandaise and French fried onion rings, of course. You can order sides of hollandaise or bearnaise sauce to go with the steak dripping in butter. So now's the time to consider one of their five salads to keep your head in the right place.

It would be, however, a mistake to eat here and not order one of their tender slabs of beef that are served on large platters, completely unadorned: *New York Strip, Filet, Petite Filet* (who are we kidding?), *Prime Rib, T-Bone,* and a "massive" *Porterhouse* for two. The menu also offers *Prime Veal Chop, Lamb Chops, Center Cut Pork Chops, BBQ Baby Back Pork Ribs, Chicken Santa Fe* (hmmmm), *Fresh Catch, Steak and Lobster,* and *Lobster Tails.* We don't need to go into dessert, do we? Well, there are eight selections if you can go on.

The lunch menu offers all the steaks plus daily specials like *Meatloaf with Green Chile* on Tuesdays, lots of salads and specialty items like *The Bull Burger* and a *Blackened Prime Rib Sandwich.*

Cafe Cassis

103 E. Water Street. 989-1717.

Executive Chef Ivan Walz

Lunch:	11 A.M..-4 P.M.. Mon.-Sat.
Dinner:	4 P.M.-10 P.M.. daily.
Brunch:	9 A.M..-3 P.M. Sat.-Sun.
Features:	Beer/Wine. Smoke-free. Patio.
Price:	Inexpensive/Moderate. Major Credit Cards.
Cuisine:	American/Italian.

*H*aagen-Dazs and Plaza Bakery owner, Fred Libby, scores again. This time with a contemporary American-style bistro inspired by regional ethnic cuisine. You'll see a lot of different chiles incorporated into many of the dishes.

The small but chic interior has twenty-foot ceilings, plenty of graceful wall hooks for those pesky coats and umbrellas, great lighting fixtures, a tiny bar facing the open kitchen where pizza dough is deftly flung into the air by white-uniformed cooks. The fantastic floor-to-ceiling, organic-shaped chimney with big, tin lizards crawling up the sides belongs to the wood-fired oven that gets those pizza crusts just right.

The diverse bistro fare has Caesar and spinach salads, a *Grilled Chicken Satay* with cold sesame noodles and vegetable springrolls served with a Habanero chile plum sauce. There are five oak-wood fired pizzas to choose from: *Green Chile Pesto Pizza* with asadero cheese, and the *Prosciutto Pizza* with marinated artichoke hearts, black olives, roasted red peppers, and Mozzarella are worth trying.

Sandwiches range from a *Cassis Club* (ask them to grill the bread for you) to the *Venison Fajita Steak Sandwich* served with red chile fries. Venison is low in fat but there are those fries. Four pastas and *Southwest Grill Blackened Salmon* dusted with achiote, cinnamon, red chile with poblano-corn relish, *Piñon Crusted Free Range Chicken Breast* with Chipotle chile-lingonberry sauce, *Vegetarian Enchiladas and Pork Medallions* complete the entrees. For dessert, try the *Warm Double Fudge Brownie* with Haagen-Dazs vanilla and raspberry coulis.

Prices are very reasonable with dinner being only a few dollars more than lunch. A big plus is that the Cafe is continuously open until 10 P.M. every night and there is a long, narrow, canvas-covered and heated patio that looks out over Water Street for people-gazing.

Cafe Escalera

❂ ❂ ❂

130 Lincoln Avenue (2nd Floor). 989-8188.

Lunch:	11:30 A.M.-2:30 P.M. Mon-Fri.
Dinner:	5:30 P.M. -9 P.M. Mon.-Thurs.;
	5:30 P.M.-10 P.M. Fri.-Sat.;
	Sunday dinners in August only: 5:30 P.M.-10 P.M.
Bar menu:	11:30 A.M.-10 P.M. Mon.-Sat.
Features:	Holiday and special menus. Smoke-free dining room.
	Full bar. Smoking permitted in bar.
	Validated parking. Art.
Price:	Moderate/Expensive. Visa/MasterCard.
Cuisine:	Mediterranean/American.

Yes, there is an escalator in Santa Fe and it's outside to boot. After the old Sears building saw its day, lucky Santa Feans witnessed the birth of one of the best restaurants in Santa Fe, Escalera, or, the "stairs." Take the escalator from Lincoln Street or the elevator from the free-for-one-hour parking lot around the block.

There's always a feeling of being special when you enter through Escalera's doors: You're immediately greeted by owner, Brian Knox, or other members of the staff, all equally capable of taking good care of you. A long zinc bar backed with a very large mirror invites you in as well. The bar area is open and light with only a low wall dividing it from the main dining area. One of the best things about the interior is that you can see just about everyone who's there, thanks to that ample bar mirror and mirrors on the outer wall.

Escalera is a meeting place for locals: a place to take your favorite client for lunch; a place to meet your friends after an art opening for drinks and dinner; a place for that special birthday lunch or dinner; and a place where Santa Fe's movers and shakers are frequently spotted. The roar of conversation and laughter results in comaraderie and good times. The best tables are positioned in front of French doors that open to the street below in the warm summer months, and are lined with pots of red geraniums. In the winter lush, velvet drapes go up to keep everything cozy.

A private dining room accommodates private parties or public events, such as the Elizabeth Berry's Heirloom Bean Tasting that occurred in 1994 and attracted all the great chefs in Santa Fe—and when necessary the doors are flung open and the room is used as an extension of the main dining room. Attention to

Cafe Escalera's Signature Dish

Pan-seared Atlantic Salmon with Horseradish Sauce

Ingredients:

4   Atlantic salmon filets, skin and bones
    removed, approximately 6 ounces each
1/2 cup light olive oil
    Zest of one lemon
    Salt and pepper to taste
    Fresh herbs: thyme, tarragon, dill,
    chives
1   small shallot, finely minced
2   tablespoons champagne vinegar
1/2 cup thick creme fraiche or sour cream
1/3 cup freshly grated horseradish

Method:

Pan-searing gives the salmon a crisp exterior and a juicy center. It could also be grilled over charcoal or broiled. Garnish the plate with tiny new potatoes, roasted beets, pickled vegetables, and watercress.

In a small bowl combine the shallot, vinegar, horseradish, salt and pepper. Let rest for 10 minutes. Fold in the creme fraiche. Check seasoning and adjust. Cover and refrigerate.

Season the salmon filets lightly with salt and pepper. Marinate the salmon with the olive oil, lemon zest and thyme for up to 6 hours.

Heat a large cast iron skillet to almost smoking, then reduce heat to medium. Lift the salmon from the marinade, letting most of the olive oil drip off but allowing the lemon zest and thyme to cling to the fish. Lay the fish in the hot pan and cook for approximately 3 minutes per side or slightly less for medium-rare. Serve with horseradish sauce on the side and scatter with freshly minced dill, tarragon and chives.

Yield: 4 servings

lovely details should be noted such as a large service table near the back of the dining room containing plates, olive oils, breads, plates of sweet butter, crisp white table linens, and wine glasses. Spectacular, year-round flower arrangements by designer Lawrence Standish grace the service table and the bar adding just the proper, elegant touch. Escalera's former chef, David Tanis, collaborated with owner Brian Knox to create a brilliant, full-flavored, Mediterranean-based menu that, thankfully, doesn't have even a tinge of New Mexican or Southwestern touches. Julia Child touted Escalera's food as straight-forward, fresh, uncomplicated, and tasty. Hip Santa Fe locals already know this and come back again and again to savor their favorite dishes. Don't be fooled by the understated menus. The many exotic and fresh ingredients used—such as locally raised organic meats and organic, heirloom produce products—from Elizabeth Berry's farm are not always listed in the short-but-sweet descriptions.

The chewy, crusty-loafed breads, whole wheat and white, ultra-fresh salads, and daily specials like *Brushettas, Wild Mushroom Ragout* with polenta, *Spring Vegetable Fricassee* with herbed spoonbread, *Spaghettini* with peas, lemon zest, basil and creme fraiche, *Curried Atlantic Salmon* with Basmati rice and yogurt raita, and *Grilled Chicken Breast* with heirloom beans, fried radicchio and olive sauce will make you a believer, too. Escalera's matchstick potatoes are exquisite—perhaps the best you've ever had.

Only the uninitiated, ("I just couldn't, Darling!") would pass on desserts. You must save room for one of the best in Santa Fe (maybe even New Mexico)—the *Blanco y Negro* is superb and the creme brulees, pots de cremes, and custards are perfection.

Cafe Oasis

526 Galisteo Street. 983-9599.

Breakfast/	
Lunch/Dinner:	9:30 A.M..-midnight Sun.-Wed.; 9:30 A.M.-2 A.M. Thurs.-Sat.
Features:	Breakfast served all day. Beer/wine. Smoking/non-smoking. Patio. Free parking lot.
Price:	Inexpensive. Visa/MasterCard.
Cuisine:	American.

*T*he neon-colored menus promise an "Oasis in the desert of life," and "For those who need magic to survive," and "Food cooked with the highest love and integrity in devotion to your body temple." There's lots of butterflies surrounding the logo of a snake coiled around the words, Cafe Oasis. (However, the "i" in Oasis is a gecko and the snake is sipping a hot drink from a cup that forms the "a" in cafe.)

The menu also states that there are "no microwave, no aluminum pots, and no fryers." This place is so "high" in energy, expect to walk out completely healed—even if you don't need to be. Vegetarians, rejoice. Although seafood, chicken, and meat are on on the menu, it should be noted that tofu and tempeh can be substituted for chicken. (Oddly enough, there are designated smoking rooms for those who haven't yet committed to a non-smoking health regimen.)

Enter in all ye who have never really left the 60s. All the typography is curvy, like the snake, and the colors are mostly bright and primary (lots of purple). The main dining area is okay—but more interesting are the different rooms painted in psychedelic colors where you and your tribe can settle in for a meal to sustain your body temple.

Cafe Pasqual's

✪ ✪ ✪

121 Don Gaspar Avenue (At Water St.). 983-9340.

Executive chef Katharine Kagel.

Breakfast:	7 A.M.-3 P.M.Mon.-Sat.
Lunch:	11 A.M.-3 P.M. Mon.-Sat.
Dinner:	6 P.M.-10:30 P.M. daily; to 10 P.M. winters only.
Sunday Brunch:	8 A.M.-2 P.M.
Features:	Beer/Wine. Smoke-free. Art.
Price:	Moderate/Expensive. Visa/MasterCard.
Cuisine:	American, Mexican, New Mexican.

*T*hey bake their own bread, churn their own ice cream, make their own chile sauces; and executive chef and owner, Katharine Kagel, has written her own cookbook, *Cafe Pasqual's,* full of "spirited recipes from Santa Fe."

Often underated, this cafe is not only one of Santa Fe's best, but it seems word-of-mouth is enough to keep it packed with locals and folks from around the world who all eagerly partake of Yucatan Mexican, New Mexican, and American cuisines.

From the outside the cafe looks funky and old with its romanticized Indian maiden posters and 30s meal signs in the windows. Inside, the smallish, two-level dining room is colorful with more of the same and stays rustic with rough, wooden tables and chairs. The decor may be basic and unrefined, but the food here is a marvel.

Cafe Pasqual's is rightly famous for its breakfasts (this is not to say that lunch and dinner are not worthy) which are served 'til 3 P.M. All the breakfast plates have mouth-watering descriptions of each, making it hard to choose just one. There's chorizo burritos, pancakes with eggs, apple-smoked bacon and pure maple syrup, omelettes, quesadillas, griddled polenta, smoked trout hash, papas fritas, and their famous *Huevos Motulenos,* a Yucatan breakfast of two over-easy eggs on blue corn tortillas with black beans topped with sauteed bananas, Feta cheese, early peas, roasted jalapeño salsa, and green chile. And, if you're lucky, individual, giant-sized fresh-fruit cobblers served with home-made ginger ice cream can appear on the breakfast or brunch menus.

Lunch and dinner have many offerings with Spanish names—it's best to take time to peruse the menus and ask your wait person for directions. The *Grilled*

Free-range Chicken Breast Sandwich with Manchego cheese, carmelized onions and jalapeños on toasted chile-cornmeal bread and cilantro pesto quesadilla are two dishes many crave for lunch—not to mention the *Corn Cakes* with sauteed calabacitas (squash) and queso blanco salsa. There's a *Grilled Salmon Burrito* with black beans, herbed goat cheese and cucumber salsa, a *Grilled Squash and Red*

Onion Enchilada with red or green chile, Monterey Jack cheese, black beans and arroz verde (green rice), salads, and the sopa del dia to give you more ideas of some of the wildly delicious food that comes out of Ms. Kagel's kitchen.

Ah, dinner. What fine morsels here? I love their *Warm French Brie* with whole-roasted garlic, jalapeño and tomatillo salsas or *Queso Fundido* (melted cheese), *de asadero* (Mexican white cow's milk cheese) *con chorizo* (spicy, pork sausage) *y tostaditas* (corn chips) to begin with. But there's so much more. Entrees boast *Chicken Mole Puebla* on Mexican rice with squash tamales and corn tortillas and two *Plato Supremo Grande's* that give you samplings of four different dishes. Don't be surprised when you find an occasional Thai listing—the *Thai Shrimp in Lemongrass-Coconut Sauce* at dinner is memorable. So is the more traditional *Grilled Rack of New Mexico Lamb* with mint-tomato salsa, sweet potato gratin, and sauteed red chard. Steak, char-grilled chicken, squash and onion enchiladas, and salmon filet show up nightly and are deftly prepared thanks to the culinary mastery of Ms. Kagel. Expert selections of wines and beers stand up to the forward flavors at Pasqual's. Sides of garlic-mashed potatoes, portobello mushrooms, and sauteed greens make savory additions to any meal.

Dessert? Of course. Here you'll find the bowl-sized *Fresh Fruit Cobbler* for sure. The *Toasted Piñon Ice Cream* with caramel sauce, *Black Walnut Tarte,* or *Double Chocolate Almond Brownie Pie* will tempt you too. Can't decide? Get the chef's dessert sampler for the table and try them all.

There's *always* a line outside the swinging screen doors—but never mind, it's well worth the wait. There's a community table for the single-minded or those that like to share space with fellow foodies.

___

Cafe Pasqual's Signature Dish

Pollo Pibil with Saffron Rice and Fire-Roasted Balsamic-Marinated Vegetables

Ingredients for the chicken:

4	teaspoons cumin seeds
1	Mexican cinnamon stick, about 3 inches
1	teaspoon whole cloves
1-1/2	tablespoons whole black peppercorns
1/2	cup achiote paste
3	tablespoons kosher salt
2	tablespoons finely minced garlic
2	cups fresh orange juice
1/2	cup fresh lime juice
2	tablespoons stemmed fresh marjoram leaves or 1 tablespoon dried
1/2	cup olive oil
6	chicken breast halves

Ingredients for the balsamic-marinated vegetables:

1	cup olive oil
1/3	cup balsamic vinegar
1	tablespoon minced garlic
2	teaspoons freshly ground black pepper
	Kosher salt
1	large red onion, sliced into thick rounds
2	red bell peppers, seeded, deveined, and cut into long strips 1/2 inch wide
2	yellow squash, sliced lengthwise into 1/4 inch-wide slabs
2	zucchini, sliced lengthwise into 1/4 inch-wide slabs
2	Japanese eggplants, sliced lengthwise into 1/4 inch-wide slabs

Method for the chicken:

Combine the cumin, cinnamon, and cloves in a small, dry sauté pan over medium heat. Roast, shaking the pan frequently, until the aromas are released, about 2 minutes. Remove from the heat and let cool. Place the spices in a spice mill or coffee grinder and grind until pulverized. Alternatively, pulverize in a mortar using a pestle. Combine all the remaining ingredients, except the chicken, in a blender or in a food processor fitted with the metal blade. Process just long enough to incorporate. Put the chicken breasts in a shallow glass dish. Pour the spice mixture evenly over the top to cover completely. Cover and place in the refrigerator to marinate for at least 24 hours or up to 36 hours, turning frequently. To prepare the marinade for the vegetables, in a bowl stir together the olive oil, vinegar, garlic, pepper, and salt to taste. Put all of the sliced vegetables in a shallow glass bowl and pour the marinade evenly over the top to coat each piece well. Marinate at room temperature for 4 to 6 hours.

Prepare a fire in a charcoal grill.

Method for the saffron rice:

Place the saffron in a small dry sauté pan over medium heat. Toast, continuously shaking the pan to prevent scorching, until fragrant, about 2 minutes. Remove from the heat and reserve. Combine the olive oil, onion, garlic, salt, and white pepper in the bottom of a large saucepan over medium heat. Stir for 1 to 2 minutes, then add the rice. Stir constantly until the oil is absorbed and the rice begins to smell nutty, 1 to 2 minutes longer. Add the water to the rice mixture, making sure that all the grains of rice are submerged and the rice is evenly distributed on the bottom of the pan. Then, add the toasted saffron and bring to a boil over medium-high heat. Reduce the heat to low, cover, and simmer until all the water is absorbed, 20 to 30 minutes.

Continued

Cafe Pasqual's Signature Dish continued:

Ingredients for the saffron rice:

1	*teaspoon saffron threads*
1/4	*cup olive oil*
1/2	*white onion, finely minced*
2	*teaspoons finely minced garlic*
1-1/2	*teaspoons kosher salt*
1/2	*teaspoon white pepper*
2	*cups long-grain white rice*
3	*cups water*

(Reprinted with permission from
Cafe Pasqual's Cookbook, Chronicle Books.)

Finish:

Remove the chicken breasts from the marinade. Arrange the breasts, skin sides down, on the grill rack about 6 inches above medium-hot coals. Grill, being careful not to overcook; this recipe should yield juicy chicken. Turn the breasts once during cooking. The cooking time depends upon the heat of the coals, the thickness of the breasts, and other variables. Plan on 15 to 20 minutes' total grilling time. Between 5 and 10 minutes before the chicken is ready, add the marinated vegetables to the grill rack. Grill, turning frequently, until charred, 7 to 12 minutes. Remove the chicken and vegetables from the grill and serve hot with saffron rice.

Yield: 6 servings

Cafe Romana

31 Burro Alley. 984-8804.

Breakfast/
Lunch/Dinner: 7:30 A.M.-4 P.M. Mon.; 7:30 A.M.-8:30 P.M.Tues.Thurs.;
 7:30 A.M.-10 P.M. Fri.-Sat.; 8:30 A.M.-9:30 P.M. Sun.
Features: Beer/wine. Smoke-free.
Price: Budget/Inexpensive. No credit cards.
Cuisine: Italian.

*L*ots of Italian/vegetarian dishes are available at this small cafe/coffeehouse located right in the heart of downtown in Santa Fe's Burro Alley. Great place to duck into after some hard-core shopping to sip one of their coffee drinks—an espresso or their version of Thai coffee (espresso sweetened with condensed milk, topped with steamed milk) or a light, low-fat lunch or snack.

Try the *House Insalata*—baby greens, Roma tomatoes and pasta topped with sweet peppers, artichokes, and goat cheese served with fresh herb vinaigrette or an anitpasti like *Mozzarella con Pomodore*—fresh Mozzarella with sun dried tomatoes, capers, artichoke hearts, fresh basil, and olives served with crostini. Of course, there's pastas galore and some of the *dolci* (sweets) can be very fine.

Carlos' Gosp'l Cafe

✪

125 Lincoln Avenue (Inside plaza at Interstate Bank Building). 983-1841.

Lunch only:	11 A.M.-4 P.M. Mon-Fri & 11 A.M.-3 P.M. Sat.
Features:	No alcohol. Smoking. Patio.
Price:	Inexpensive. No credit cards.
Cuisine:	American.

Photo by Matt Gray

Continuously playing gospel music, sofa-funk seating, and a pay-as-you-leave trust system, set the stage for this happy-go-lucky cafe.

Surprisingly, there are still folks out there who don't know about Carlos's famous *Hangover Stew* (a spicy potato, corn, and green chile chowder with Monterey Jack cheese) that will set you right after a night out. Lip-smacking fat sandwiches with sassy names (the *Alice B. Toklas* is fresh turkey breast with Swiss cheese, tomato, onions, avocado, sprouts, and mayo; or the *Miles Standish,* fresh turkey breast with cranberries, cream cheese, and mayonnaise; or the *Jack Dempsey,* roast beef, Cheddar cheese, red onion, lettuce, tomato, mustard, mayo, and horseradish), and tasty house-made potato salad are available daily. My favorite meal here is a bowl of Hangover Stew, a half sandwich of the *New Mexican Meatloaf* with green chile, Cheddar and all the trimmings, and a slice of baked-fresh-daily lemon meringue pie.

The menu heading for desserts says, "Say Amen Desserts." Now that the secret's out, boogie on down for a down-home treat and do what you're told: say Amen.

Coyote Cafe

✪ ✪ ✪

132 W. Water Street. 983-1615.

Executive Chef Mark Kiffin

Lunch:	11:30 A.M.-1:45 P.M. Mon.-Fri.
Dinner:	6 P.M.-9:30 P.M. Sun.-Thurs.;
	5:30 P.M.-9:45 P.M. Fri.-Sat.
Brunch:	11:30 A.M.-1:45 P.M. Sat.-Sun.
Features:	Full bar. Smoke-free dining room.
	Smoking permitted in bar. Art.
Price:	Expensive/Very Expensive. Major credit cards.
Cuisine:	Southwestern.

*W*hat becomes a cafe-legend most? In this case it's owner Mark Miller, *bon vivant*, and high priest of the new Southwestern cuisine, who has created this restaurant with a mix of food philosophy: Tex-Mex, Pueblo Indian, Hispanic-New Mexican, and Berkeley—food mecca, USA. Celebrities and out-of-towners mostly flock to the Temple Coyote to pay homage to what is heralded as the best-in-the-west, nouvelle Southwestern cuisine.

Some locals feel it's the restaurant they love to hate but many have come 'round to the side of love. The outlandish interior features contemporary, kinetic sculptures by artist, Frederick Prescott, a menagerie of life-size, wild animal sculptures high overhead, bright colors, painted floors, and an open kitchen situated in front of the bar where you can watch part of your meal being prepared. While you're waiting for dinner, saddle up a barstool (chairs and barstools covered in, yes, real cowhide) and ask for a *Brazilian Daiquiri* (blended rums with fresh pineapple and vanilla beans) or a *Chile-tini* (chile-infused vodka on the rocks with a jalapeño tomatillo). Don't pass up the chance to get a side order of Coyote's famous *Red Chile Onion Rings* while you're imbibing.

Dinner decisions forthcoming, consider one of Chef Mark Kiffin's signature dishes: For an appetizer, order *Chipotle Shrimp* with buttermilk corn cakes, Pico de Gallo Salsa on the side. Or for your main entree try the 22-ounce, bone-in, aged prime rib *Cowboy Steak* heaped with onion rings—enough beef here to satisfy hardy cowboys and girls and armchair buckaroos. It almost doesn't matter what you order here, it will be unique, creative, visually interesting, flavorful, and downright hot—and I don't mean stove hot. Elizabeth Berry's superior organic produce is used as much as possible although this isn't always mentioned on the menu.

Desserts at the Coyote are good, so loosen up those belts, cowhands, and dig into Andrew MacLauchlan's *Caramelized McIntosh Abiquiu Apple* with burnt honey ice cream and gingered Alamogordo quince sauce. If you're a chocolate fiend, go for the *Chocolate Thunder*—just order it. The wines, port, Madeira, sherries, cognacs, armagnac, and calvados listed on the dessert menu can be overwhelming so ask your competent waiter for suggestions.

If your wallet is wincing, go for lunch or brunch, and you'll still enjoy lots of Coyote Cafe's creative food.

Coyote Cafe's Signature Dish

Chipotle Shrimp with Corn Cakes and Pico de Gallo Salsa

Ingredients for the shrimp:

1-1/2   *pounds medium shrimp (about 30)*
3   *tablespoons butter*

Ingredients for the chipotle butter:

1   *cup softened butter*
4-1/2   *tablespoons canned chipotle chiles, pureed*
1-1/2   *dozen corn cakes (recipe follows)*
2   *green onions, chopped*
1   *cup Pico de Gallo Salsa (recipe follows)*

Ingredients for corn cakes:

3/4   *cup all-purpose flour*
1/2   *cup coarse cornmeal (polenta)*
1/2   *teaspoon baking powder*
1/2   *teaspoon baking soda*
1   *teaspoon salt*
1   *teaspoon sugar*
1-1/4   *cups buttermilk*
2   *tablespoons melted butter*
1   *egg, beaten*
1   *cup fresh corn kernels*
1   *green onion, chopped*

Method:

Peel the shrimp. On a griddle or in a frying pan, cook the shrimp in 3 tablespoons butter over low heat for about 5 minutes, turning them once.

To prepare chipotle butter, roughly puree together the softened butter and 1-1/2 tablespoons chipotle puree and set aside at room temperature.

Method:

Place the dry ingredients in a bowl and mix together. In a large bowl, whisk the buttermilk and butter together and then whisk in the egg. Gradually add the dry ingredients to the liquid and whisk until thoroughly incorporated. Puree 1/2 cup of the corn, and fold it into the batter along with the whole kernels and green onions. Add a little buttermilk if necessary to thin the mixture.

Using a nonstick pan over medium heat, ladle corn cake batter and form 3-inch cakes. Cook until golden brown (about 2-1/2 minutes on each side.) Batter makes about 18 to 20 corn cakes.

Continued

Coyote Cafe's Signature Dish continued:

Ingredients for Pico de Gallo Salsa:

2	*tablespoons diced onion*
2	*cups tomatoes chopped into*
	1/4 inch cubes
2	*serrano chiles, finely chopped*
2	*tablespoons finely chopped cilantro*
2	*teaspoons sugar*
1/4	*cup Mexican beer*
2	*teaspoons salt*
	Juice of 1 lime

(Reprinted with permission from *Coyote Cafe*, Mark Miller, Ten Speed Press.)

Method:

Put onion in a strainer, rinse with hot water, and drain. Combine all ingredients and mix well. Let sit in the refrigerator for at least 30 minutes before serving. Feel free to consume the rest of the beer while waiting!

Finish:

Place 3 corn cakes on each plate. Place 5 shrimp on top of the cakes and spread the chipotle butter liberally over the shrimp. Sprinkle the chopped green onions over the shrimp. Serve the Pico de Gallo salsa at the side of the corn cakes.

Yield: 6 servings

Coyote Cafe Rooftop Cantina

❂ ❂

132 W. Water Street. 983-1615

Lunch/Dinner: **11:30 A.M.-9:30 P.M. daily. May through October.**
Features: **Full bar. Smoking permitted. Outdoor seating only.**
Price: **Inexpensive/Moderate. Major credit cards.**
Cuisine: **Mexican.**

*T*he Coyote Cafe's answer to a Mexican cantina: festive, casual, bustling, unstuffy, and lot's of fun. Located in the heart of the old downtown area, this is the perfect place to stop in for snacks, a full meal, or drinks.

You must go into the Coyote Cafe's entrance, up the stairs and through the door on the left to the outside. One of Prescott's more fanciful moving sculptures greets you as you climb a few more stairs and get to the right spot. There are no reservations here but the wait is usually not long. Most of the tight seating is under heavy canvas awnings to protect diners from the sun and summer thunderstorms that can kick up without much warning. And under-the-sky seating overlooks the balcony wall onto Water Street for more people watching.

The mood is quick-paced. Gaggles of servers are practically running around the tables balancing trays laden with refreshing drinks like *Penafiels* (Mexican sodas). Other non-alcoholic "summer coolers" include their *Fresh Lemon Lime Liquado* which is a must and pairs perfectly with the spicy hot cuisine. Cocktail lovers won't be dissapointed: The *Brazilian Daiquiri* (made famous by their parent cafe, Coyote) with a blend of rums, fresh pineapple and Mexican vanilla beans is served on the rocks or there's the *Sun-burnt Señorita*—a margarita made with fresh watermelon juice (my favorite) or the *Sangria* with red wine, tropical fruits, and Juniper berries—olé! Of course there is a nice selection of cervezas frias (beers) like Negra Modelo, Santa Fe Pale Ale, Rolling Rock, and Buckler (NA).

Once the drink order is in, it's time to make hard decisions from the menu because everything sounds mouth-watering, and it is. The *Griddled Buttermilk Corncakes* with Chipotle shrimp and salsa fresca is wonderful; so is the *Queso Fundido Con Chorizo*—a dish served all over Mexico City, in low and high-end restaurants, that easily serves two as an appetizer. If you're not already familiar with this traditional Mexican dish, it's a melted blend of cheeses and spicy sausages served bubbling hot in a flat dish with a warm stack of flour tortillas on the side for scooping up the savory mixture.

The *Coyote's Caesar Salad,* small or large, is worth ordering: Perfectly fresh and crisp Romaine, Caesar dressing, freshly grated Parmesan and garlic croutons make for a light lunch or a delicious first course. Try the *Spicy Tortilla Soup* dolloped with Cilantro crema, another traditional Mexican dish. Under the headings of *Cantina Specialties and Traditional Favorites* the choices get rather difficult but you can't make a mistake. How about *Red Chile Honey-Glazed Ruby Red Trout* served with tropical fruit salsa, rice and beans or the *Barbecued Pork Chops*—two marinated pork chops grilled with orange barbecue sauce, serrano slaw and beans. The ever-popular *¡La Cubana!* is the legendary Coyote sandwich made with sliced pork loin, ham, guacamole, Chipotle chile, Jack cheese, and a spicy black bean spread. The *Barbecued Duck Quesadilla* runs a close second in popularity and you can have it with a small green salad and salsa.

Cool your palate down with one of the Rooftop's sumptuous desserts like *Cajeta Caramel Sundae* with vanilla ice cream and toasted Piñons (Cajeta is a thick caramel made from sheep's or cow's milk found everywhere in Mexico), or the *Mexican Coffee Flan.*

Plus: The Cantina menu moves inside the Coyote Cafe for the winter, serving all the above favorites for lunch from 11:30 A.M.-1:45 P.M.

Evangelo's Mediterranean Cafe

229 Galisteo Street. 820-6526.

Chef: Zorba

Lunch/Dinner: 11 A.M.-11:30 P.M. Mon.-Sat.;
               11 A.M.-10:30 P.M. Sun.
Features: Full bar. Smoking/non-smoking. Patio.
Price: Inexpensive/Moderate. Visa/MasterCard.
Cuisine: Greek.

I have waited very patiently for Greek food to arrive in Santa Fe. In the past, whenever I flew to San Diego to visit my daughter, the first planned food outing was to quickly go to our favorite Greek restaurant and order the Gyro Platter which immediately quelled the cravings I had carried around for months in New Mexico. Now I can pop into Evangelo's Mediterranean Cafe and get my Greek or, I should say, my Gyro-fix.

Let's get one thing straight: Gyro is pronounced YEE-roh by the Greeks. So if you hear anyone pronouncing it like jiros as in the word, gryrate, muffle your laughter and proudly order up with the correct pronunciation. *Gyro* is a Greek specialty: Minced lamb is formed into a long cylinder, wrapped and molded around a vertical spit that turns the lamb slowly around so it is roasted by the burners until the outside of the meat forms a wonderful brown crust that enfolds the juicy meat within. The crusty, outside meat is thinly sliced right off the spit for Gyro sandwiches or dinner platters. Even die-hard lamb haters will like this one.

Evangelo's serves up a remarkedly good Gryo sandwich called the *Kronos Gyro* that is garnished with the traditional tomatoes, onions, and tzatziki sauces (yogurt, cucumber, garlic, and olive oil). All this is wrapped up with the lamb in a proper pocketless pita. (The superior pocketless pitas are hard to find in New Mexico but they are well worth the search if you do find them.) Oddly enough, the Gyro is served with bland French fries and a non-descript salad with bits of Feta cheese and a couple of tomato wedges. The salad was dry and seemed to lack any kind of dressing. A drizzle of olive oil and a squeeze of lemon would have helped it 100 percent. One of the owners assured me that the French fries were only temporary until a more authentic side dish was selected to take their place.

Evangelo's menu is short and simple reflecting the kitchen's effort to make most dishes in-house and as fresh as possible. Besides the Gyro, there's *Mama's Lemon Chicken, Pastitsio, Souvlaki, Tiropita, Spanokopita,* and *dolmas* on the lunch menu.

At dinner, several appetizers or meze (meh ZAY) appear such as *Taramosalata* (fish roe, olive oil, garlic and lemon) and *Htapodi* (octopus marinated in olive oil, vinegar, and lemon sauce)—two appetizers you don't find just anywhere. Zorba, the "chef," has added charcoal broiled *Baby Lamb Chops, Skapia La Greka,* shrimp topped with lemon white sauce, and *Zorba Shrimp,* a dish that is made with Feta cheese and tomatoes.

All the side dishes accompanying the entrees are so-so and the kitchen needs to work on developing more interesting ones. I suggest you order the *Oretiko,* a sampling of appetizers, or ask the wait staff to bring a side plate of Feta cheese, Greek olives, tomatoes, and olive oil in lieu of the French fries.

Zorba has outdone himself with the one dessert that is featured on the menu— *Baklavas.* Obviously made with loving hands, this baklava is dripping with syrup, chock full of almonds, sugar, and cinnamon—very rich and sweet—just the way I like it. The generous portion can easily be shared by two or in my case, easily devoured by one.

It wouldn't be a Greek meal if you didn't order up Ouzo for an aperitif. The bar stocks Metaxa Ouzo, a peppery 90-proof-strong, clear liqueur with sweet, mild anise flavors. Ask for a glass of water on the side and mix in the Ouzo—it turns whitish and opaque, like Pernod. And definitely order a glass or bottle of Boutari Retsina Greek wine with your meal. It's perfect with Greek food.

Evangelo's space is light and cheery, in hues of white and blue. There are busts of Greek gods, goddesses, and philosophers, high ceilings, and oversized paned-windows that are flung open in summer to let in a view of the sky and the lovely, sunny patio.

The French Pastry Shop

---

100 San Francisco Street (At La Fonda Hotel). 983-6697.

Breakfast/	
Lunch:	**7 A.M.-5 P.M. daily.**
Features:	**No alcohol. Smoke-free.**
Price:	**Budget. No credit cards. Cash only.**
Cuisine:	**French.**

With his tan, bald head bobbing about and his thick French accent exclaiming *bon jour* Madame or Monsieur, owner George Zadeyan could charm the socks off anyone. He's been greeting people from all over the world since 1974 as they enter his little cafe for excellent French pastries, breads, roll, and quiches.

The interior has the flavor of an old French country inn with dark, heavy woods, lots of old brick, and hefty chandeliers. The menu is small but has all the requirements of a French bakery.

Crepes as Meal starts out the listings that are written on a large board hanging behind pastry cases. Standards are egg, ham, and cheese, ratatouille, spinach with or without chicken, and chicken-mushroom. *Croque Monsieur* or *Madame*, ham and cheese, salami, turkey, and beef fill the bill for sandwiches—don't expect the American type—French sandwiches are much simpler.

The *Tourte Milanaise* and perfect *Quiche Lorraine* are also available to take home—whole or by the wedge. *Crepes as Dessert* using fruits in season are a delight. And if your sweet tooth is still aching, try a fruit tart, chocolate eclair or mousse, or one of the traditional pastries of France: *Montmarte, St. Michel, Opera,* or *Napolean.* A raspberry cookie the size of a small plate are displayed in the cases along with buttery, flaky puff pastry rolls such as *croissant, palmier,* and *apple tart.*

Don't forget to pick up a baguette on the way out when you bid George *au revoir.*

Galisteo News

201 Galisteo Street. 984-1316.

Breakfast/	
Lunch/Snacks:	7 A.M.-7 P.M. **Sun.-Thurs.; 7 A.M.-11 P.M. Fri.-Sat.**
Features:	**No alcohol. Smoking-non-smoking. Patio.**
Price:	**Budget/Inexpensive. No credit cards.**
Cuisine:	**American.**

With a patio located on a key corner of downtown (Galisteo and Water Streets) this could be the best coffeehouse for people-gawking. Shoppers from home and abroad stroll this area in multitudes under the watchful, sunglassed-eyes of Galisteo News' customers lolling outside in the sun.

Not only was Galisteo News the first coffeehouse-magazine stand in Santa Fe, it has enjoyed a loyal following since it opened in the early 80s. It has a fine selection of magazines and serves robust coffees, sandwiches, pastries, and desserts, as well as fancy teas in the tea room.

Grant Corner Inn

122 Grant Street. 983-6678.

Breakfast:	8 A.M.-9 A.M. **Mon-Fri.**
Brunch:	8 A.M.-10:30 A.M. **Sat & 8 A.M.-1 P.M. Sun.**
Features:	**No alcohol. Smoke-free.**
	Reservations are recommended at all times listed.
Price:	**Inexpensive. Visa/MasterCard.**
Cuisine:	**American.**

You'll feel as is you've just stepped back to a more genteel time when you have breakfast here. If you're not a guest of the Inn, you *must* call ahead for reservations.

Summertime is best, when the old-fashioned, shady veranda is available for outside seating and the smell of fresh-brewed coffee wafts through the warm air. Sample their homemade pastries, jellies, granolas, waffles, and daily special entrees. (Think about booking a room for the total experience in this charming bed and breakfast inn.)

Haagen-Daz Ice Cream Shoppe/ Plaza Bakery

56 E. San Francisco Street. 988-3858.

Breakfast/	
Lunch/Dinner:	**7 A.M.-11 P.M. daily. To 10:30 P.M. in winter.**
Features:	**No alcohol. Smoke-free.**
Price:	**Budget/Inexpensive. No credit cards.**
Cuisine:	**American.**

*S*equestered snugly on the southwest corner of Santa Fe's old, historic Plaza, this place has the honor of being the most visited Haagen-Dazs Ice Cream store in America.

Not only can you get your favorite hand-packed Haagen-Dazs (Coffee Chip is still only available hand-packed), but the owners have wisely installed a bakery on the premises that turns out croissants—sweet and savory, pizzas, breads, and some of the best pastries, pies, cakes, and other sweets in town. Don't forget—you can get their famous ice cream pies, prepared daily. Of course there are sandwiches, salads, and soups as well.

"Two scoops of French Vanilla in a sugar cone, please."

Hotel St. Francis

210 Don Gaspar Avenue. 983-5700.

Afternoon Tea:	3 P.M.-5:30 P.M. daily.
Features:	Full bar. Open to 2 A.M. Mon.-Sat.; to midnight Sun. Smoking/non-smoking. [Historical]
Price:	Budget/Inexpensive. Major credit cards.
Cuisine:	English Tea.

*A*fternoon tea is an old tradition that is luckily being kept alive in the lobby of the Hotel St. Francis. This lobby is one of the "grande dame" of lobbies. When you enter, you'll see why.

High ceilings, deep red-tiled floors polished to a high sheen, ironwork chandeliers, elegant columns, dark woods, antiques, antique reproductions, oriental rugs, potted Ficus trees, soft lighting, and Victorian fringed table lamps all set the stage for old-world elegance. Colors of muted rust-burgundy and teal-blues show up on the over-sized, comfortable wingback chairs and sofas arranged to encourage intimate conversations. As you enter to the left, a stunning stone fireplace — with a bas-relief of dancing cherubs—blazes in the winter months keeping you warm inside while the snow falls. The concierge said the fireplace was hidden behind a wall for years until it was accidently discovered by workmen during a recent remodeling.

Tables are set up for tea all around the large room so you can choose to be next to windows or the fireplace. The tea-for-two settings near the fire are lovely. Tea service is British-style and a *full tea* of assorted finger sandwiches, a scone with cream and strawberry jam, a pastry and, of course, a pot of tea is offered as well as a tea with just the scone.

Tea selections include *Darjeeling Margaret's Hope GFOP* from the Himalayas, *St. Francis Blend* of Darjeeling and Chinese teas with essence of passion fruit, *Earl Grey* from China with oil of bergamot, *Passion Fruit*, smokey *Oolong* from China, *Flavored Black Teas, Herbal Teas,* and *English Breakfast*. My choice is always Earl Grey.

In the summer the hotel's veranda that looks out on the passing parade is ever so cooling—and you just might see a full moon rise up over the town while sipping iced tea or a cocktail before the Opera. It's, oh, so civilized my dear.

India Palace

---

227 Don Gaspar Avenue. 986-5859.

Lunch Buffet:	11:30 A.M.-2:30 P.M. daily.
Dinner:	5 P.M.-10 P.M. daily.
Features:	Beer/wine. Smoke-free. Patio. Validated parking.
Price:	Moderate/Expensive. Major credit cards.
Cuisine:	East Indian.

*T*here is a scene from David Lean's movie, *Passage to India,* where Indian characters are ready to begin their meal. A cloth that has been covering a large area on a low table is lifted up with a dramatic flourish, to reveal the elegant mystery beneath—aromatic, ambrosial Indian food. Food meant to be enjoyed by all the human senses. When the cloth is removed, the actors inhale deeply and cry out with delight before beginning a meal that epitomizes one of the world's finest cuisines. When the movie moves to a food scene involving the British intruders, they gloomily munch on cucumber sandwiches and boiled beef.

Indian cuisine is distinguished by its sensuous nature. It has a complexity of textures and heady flavors that range from delicate to intense, cool to hot, creamy to dry, sweet to salty, thick to thin, crunchy to smooth.

Santa Fe is lucky to have a restaurant that serves this cuisine. India Palace features Eastern Indian food (the type Americans are most familiar with) with chef Bal Dev Sigh at the helm. The best way to enjoy Indian food is a la carte, so keep this in mind when ordering.

Papadum (extremely thin, crispy cracker-bread made with lentil flour) is brought out in a basket with two complementary dipping sauces—one a thin, mild, sweetish deep red-brown sauce and the other a thick, spicy pale-green yogurt-based sauce. Definitely order Indian *nan* (bread) to start or go with your meal. Nan is a lightly leavened flat bread baked in a Tandoor oven by slapping a circle of the dough up against the volcano-hot oven wall where it puffs up, takes on a slighty smokey flavor, and is done in 60-seconds. (The Tandoor is a tall, round clay oven fired by wood or charcoal that reaches 800 degrees Fahrenheit. Chicken will cook in five minutes so it demands skillful knowledge to be able to master the Tandoor.) The stuffed nans are really delicious. Try the *Kashmiri Nan* stuffed with cashews, pistachios, raisins, and cherries. Before ordering the main meal try to think about different textures, flavors, and aromas so you can enjoy the complete breadth of symmetry that's so indicative of Indian food.

All the rice dishes are infused with exotic saffron. *Peas Pallao* (rice with green peas) or the *Vegetable Buryani Rice* with veggies and nuts) are divine. There are nine *Tandoori Specialties*—you must have at least one: lamb, jumbo prawns, chicken, mixed grill, and marinated fish are some excellent choices. *Masalas* (tomato sauce), *curries, vindaloos* (hot spicy sauce with potatoes), *kormas* (mild cream sauce with cashews, almonds, and raisins), *sags* (spinach-based), and *dals* (lentils) are de-scribed beautifully on the menu and overlap the poultry, meats, seafood, and veg-etable sections. Good side order choices are the *Raita* (cooling yogurt with cu-cumber, tomatoes, and mint) and *Mango Chutney.*

Indian desserts are designed to cool and refresh your palate and Indian Palace has some good ones. I particularly enjoyed *Kulfi,* a house-made ice cream with pistachios and almonds. I won't leave an Indian restaurant without having an order of *Gulab Jamun*—a dessert that's hard to describe. But think of a baba (a cake soaked in rum syrup) in the shape of doughnut holes and you're close. The Gulab Jamun (little tender, juicy, milk-based balls soaked in sweet saffron syrup) creates a perfect ending to an illustrious meal. Some find Indian desserts too sweet. But realize that Indians believe that the last thing to linger on your lips should be . . . sweetness.

Josie's Casa de Comida

225 E. Marcy Steet. 983-5311.

Lunch:	11 A.M.-3 P.M. Mon-Fri.
Features:	No alcohol. Smoke-free. [Historical]
Price:	Inexpensive. No credit cards.
Cuisine:	New Mexican.

*E*nter into Josie's white cottage and try some very casual New Mexican: stacked or rolled enchiladas smothered in Josie's great red chile (meat or meatless) with an egg on top. Everything is cooked to order so there may be a bit of a wait.

Don't even think of leaving without trying a slab of one of Josie's fresh fruit pies or cobblers, or a slice of mocha cake—all slathered with real whipped cream.

The fame of this place has spread far and wide over the past twenty-six years. Even so, locals bemoaned the fact that after Josie Gallegos closed down for a few months (the rumor was that she just got tired), the menu and decor changed from eccentric-funk to sterile, middle-class. But do not fear, the limited menu is still, *real* Josie.

Julian's

⊗ ⊗

221 Shelby Street. 988-2355.

Chef/co-owner Wayne Gustafson

Dinner:	**6 P.M.-10:30 P.M.daily.**
Features:	**Full bar. Smoke-free. Patio.**
Price:	**Moderate/Expensive. Major credit cards.**
Cuisine:	**Italian. (Menu changes seasonally.)**

Regional Italian food, featuring some Tuscan cuisine, soft, piped-in jazz, art deco stained glass, twinkling lights, enormous mirrors, glowing-ochre walls, candlelight, and several kiva fireplaces make this one romantic spot for dinner.

For starters try the *Melanzane alla Griglia con Peperoni* (eggplant grilled with olive oil and roasted red peppers and balsamic vinegar)—it's delicious, low in fat, and visually beautiful; the *Petto di Pollo in Agro Dolce* entree (boneless breast of chicken sauteed with raisins, shallots, and capers in a sweet and sour wine sauce) is unusual and practically addictive.

The assortment of pastas includes some well-known classics and chef Gustafson's repeatedly requested *Polenta con Funghi al' Ungherese* (portobello, oyster, shiitake mushrooms and spinach sauteed with Marsala wine, paprika and cream, served with soft polenta cooked with fontina cheese). This dish is available in the winter months only.

There's a nice selection of *dolci* and of course espresso, cappuccino, and an extensive list of Italian and California wines.

That's *amore*.

Julian's Signature Dish

Polenta con Funghi al' Ungherese

Ingredients for polenta:

2   cups milk
2   cups water
     Salt and pepper
1   cup coarse ground cornmeal
1/2 cup Fontina cheese, diced

Method:

Bring milk and water to a boil, add salt and pepper, sprinkle in the cornmeal stirring constantly to avoid lumps. Cook on low heat stirring occasionally until the mixture begins to thicken. Stir in the fontina. Divide among four plates.

Ingredients for the Funghi al' Ungherese:

1-1/2 pounds mixed mushrooms chopped
       or sliced—portobello, shiitake, or oyster
4   tablespoons butter
1/4   cup sweet Marsala
1/4   cup heavy cream
1   tablespoon paprika

Method:

While the polenta is cooking, sauté the mushrooms in butter. When nearly cooked, add the marsala and bring to boil. Add the paprika, salt, pepper, and cream. Stir and continue simmering until the sauce is slightly thickened and the mushrooms are completely cooked. Serve over the polenta.

Yield: 4 servings

La Casa Sena

⭐ ⭐

125 East Palace Street. 988-9232.

Executive chef John Kelly Rogers
Sous chef Bruce Kalman

Lunch:	11:30 A.M.-3 P.M. daily.
Dinner:	5:30 P.M.-10 P.M. daily.
Cantina Menu:	5 P.M.-10 P.M. daily.
Features:	Full bar. Smoke-free inside. Smoking permitted on patio. Art. [Historical]
Price:	Expensive/Very expensive. Major credit cards.
Cuisine:	Regional Southwestern. (Menu changes seasonally.)

*T*his historic building was built for a bride—Major Jose Sena's—back in 1860. If you come for nothing else, sit in the old brick courtyard that now serves as the restaurant's outdoor dining room. It's probably one of the coolest spots in midsummer when the sun is coming down hard on hatless heads, and you're longing for a tall, cool drink. Aim for the can't-miss Alice-in-Wonderland umbrella that's surrounded by a lush display of flowers, mammoth cottonwood trees, a bubbling fountain...and chill out.

The restaurant's building is a visually stunning example of 19th century Territorial-style adobe architecture. Inside, ceilings soar to fifteen-feet in the center dining room, but are low and intimate in three other cozy dining rooms. The vigas and columns are old and enormous, and the four chandeliers are magnificent tin constructions. Lighting is soft, and there's a central fireplace for chilly evenings. Starched, white tablecloths on heavy wood tables are accented with big napkins, folded and placed in wine glasses. The many details and attention to place settings set the mood for fine dining. Waiters, in white shirts and ties, are there to be genuinely helpful.

When you make your reservations, be sure to mention that you'd like to be put in the capable hands of manager, Joseph Biggert. As he would say: "If you let me drive the boat, you'll be happy."

There are two ways to approach dinner: One is to go with the evening's *Chef Tasting Menu*, or order a la carte from the dinner menu. The *Chef Tasting Menu* offers a five course dinner that begins with *Santa Fe Market Salad* and ends with a chef's selection of desserts—so bring a healthy appetite and plan at least two hours at the table. Since this menu changes every evening, it's a good idea to ask about the new menu when you call. If Joseph is your guide, a delightful version of a pupu boat (the Hawaiian term for any cold or hot appetizer) might show up

before the salad. The pupus are cleverly served in a wine-box on a bed of fresh lavender strewn with flower petals. The night we dined, the pupus nestled in the box were soft-shelled crabs drizzled with serrano aioli, fat Portobello mushrooms sandwiched between house-made English muffins the size of silver dollars, and rock shrimp seviche on tiny blinis with pickled ginger on the side.

Joseph selected our wine from La Casa Sena's extraordinary wine cellar. He started us out with a *1992 Le Montrachet Grand Cru, Remoissenet Pere & Fils,* then followed it up with the oldest label in the cellar, a bottle of *1981 Vosne-Romanee Les Orveaux,* a Bordeaux from the Robert Haas Selection. Magnificent!

First courses from the dinner menu are flavorful and fanciful: *Upside Down Caesar Salad Pizzetta* with red chile-lime dressing, aged Jack cheese, roasted garlic chips, and sundried tomatoes could be your number one choice; or perhaps the *Lobster Piki Roll* with vinegar-spiked Nappa cabbage slaw, mango sweet and sour sauce, wasabi mustard and Asian shrimp salsa. If the *Sesame and Scallion Shrimp Tempura* with slaw is available, get it. It's light as a feather and delicious.

I highly recommend the *Intermezzo* with a choice of either an ice-cold, mouth-watering, and cleansing watermelon-jalapeño, or grapefruit-serrano granita.

Entrees like the *Pan Seared Molasses Duck Breast* with blackberry and port wine sauce, potato-thyme pancake and southwestern stir-fry; or *Pistachio-crusted Chilean Sea Bass Napoleon* with tangerine hot and sour sauce, tatsoi greens, charred tomatillo aioli and choyote squash stir-fry; or *Grilled Corn-fed American Rack of Lamb Chops* with habanero-papaya "faya" tropical fruit salsa and crispy root vegetable chips—reveal mastery in the kitchen with the complex pairing of meats, fish, chiles, fruits, and vegetables.

La Plazuela and Bell-Tower Bar

100 East San Francisco Street. (La Fonda Hotel) 982-5511.

Breakfast:	7 A.M.-10:45 A.M. daily.
Lunch:	11:15 A.M.-2 P.M. Mon.-Fri.; 11:15 A.M.-3 P.M. Sat.-Sun.
Dinner:	5:30 P.M.-10 P.M.daily.
Bell-Tower Bar:	4 P.M.-8:30 P.M. Mon.-Thurs.; 2 P.M.-8:30 P.M. Fri-Sun.
Features:	Full Bar. Smoke-free. Art. [Historical]
Price:	Moderate/Expensive. Major credit cards.
Cuisine:	Continental/New Mexican.

The La Fonda Hotel remains a self-assured cornerstone of history for Santa Fe, resting at the end of Old Santa Fe Trail. Visitors from all over the world come here to bask in the hotel's notoriety and rich Spanish heritage.

A sight to behold, the bustling lobby alone is worth a visit with its tiled floors, gigantic armchairs, high-viga ceilings, dark woods, and Gerald Cassidy paintings from 1922. Ghosts of tenants-past, in framed pictures, seem to roam the halls and brush past you in dimly-lit corridors. Famous guests have included Pat Garrett, Billy the Kid, General Sherman, Ulysses S. Grant, and Kit Carson.

The best thing about La Fonda's only restaurant isn't the food. It's the restaurant's location in an indoor, enclosed courtyard that floods diners with light from a skylight high above.

La Plazuela may be fine for one meal. But like a lot of old classic restaurants in Santa Fe, this one is also being usurped by newer, more innovative food places run by first-rate chefs. Even though you can get better New Mexican cuisine for half the price elsewhere, La Plazuela remains a favorite place to eat for those who have kept alive romantic memories of their visits here year after year.

The Bell-Tower Bar is located on the roof of La Fonda and continues to be a rendezvous point for drinks. And sunsets here might be the best you've ever seen.

The Old House

✪ ✪

309 West San Francisco Street. (At the Eldorado Hotel.)
988-4455.

Executive Chef Phillip Kephart.

Dinner only: 5:30 P.M.-10 P.M. Tues.-Sun.
Features: Full bar. Smoking/non-smoking [Historical]
Price: Expensive/Very expensive. Major credit cards.
Cuisine: New Southwestern. (Menu changes weekly.)

𝒀ou may roll your eyes when you see the over-blown size of The Eldorado Hotel—it seems entirely out of perspective with the Santa Fe aesthetic—and it is! Even so, this hotel gathers in the rich and famous from all over the world. And it must be said that the hotel harbors a wonderful restaurant, The Old House, still pretty much a dining secret to locals who generally avoid hotel restaurants.

It's called The Old House because this is the original site of a 100-year-old adobe building. But instead of tearing it down, the developers, who thought their hearts were in the right place, just covered it all over so that not a suggestion of it remains. In any event, the restaurant that now occupies this space has reintroduced their patrons to the genteel art of dining, start to finish.

Arriving without reservations won't faze the staff here—their utmost desire is to please and make sure you have a pleasurable, if not memorable, meal. The larger, main dining room is smoke-free, has a fireplace, a grand piano, and is pleasant enough. But my favorite dining room is the small, intimate Wine Cellar Room—set aside for the restaurant's extensive wines and lucky smokers who usually get the less desirable eating spaces these days. Throw caution to the wind if you've quit (smoking, that is) and ask to get seated here. (This room is often reserved for special parties, so call ahead.) Low light provided by flickering votives perched on old moorish doors conceals the wine storage. The chairs are *real* dining chairs, so comfortable you can actually spend several hours sitting without worrying about back trouble later. Large, glass-topped tables that were once heavy wood doors show off East Indian grillwork underneath. The whole room whispers romance. Don't be surprised if your waitperson brings out several bottles of house wine for a mini-tasting to help make those pre-dinner wine selections.

Another lovely surprise is the on-the-house appetizer that promptly shows up on the table: Made-in-house *Sesame Lavosh Crackers* with a little tub of *Chipotle-*

honey cream cheese. Before main entrees arrive a generous bowl of fresh greens is presented at the table where your wait person prepares the dressing and salad tableside—included with your entrees. It's a delicious combination of Romaine and red leaf lettuce, yellow peppers, jícama, Roma tomatoes, and a queso cotija (mild, fresh white cheese) and *Balsamic vinegar vinaigrette.* Also, two butters, a sweet maple corriander and a savory-spicy prickly pear, are served with a basket of good breads to stave off any hunger you still may be experiencing.

You can't go wrong with superb appetizers like *Southwestern Blackened Shrimp* with orange cilantro sauce. And the unexpected *Rattlesnake* (farm-fat grown, no bones) sauteed with green chile dust, served with red posole, sweet corn, arugula, and sundried tomato sauce is an appetizer you'll *dare* to order.

One of the best lamb dishes in Santa Fe is right here. The *Old House Rack of Lamb* with pepita-roasted garlic crust, stuffed with Feta cheese, sundried tomatoes, and black olives is sensational; so is the *House-smoked Antelope* (the Antelope is shaved thin and served with penne pasta, wild mushrooms, arugula, red pepper and roasted garlic Anaheim chile sauce). Game expert, Roxanne Malone, said it was one of the best Antelope dishes she's ever tasted, and she has cooked and tasted a great many.

Now is not the time to shy away from the dessert tray. The desserts are presented fashioned out of butter to keep them picture perfect on the tray. But when the real thing is set before you, you know you've done the correct thing. The fun-loving, deep-fried, banana-filled chimichanga with chocolate sauce and Ben & Jerry's Chunky Monkey Ice Cream is a hoot! Service is professional and knowledgeable (some over-the-top wait-jargon might put you off but this is a minor *faux pas*). Courses are well paced leaving just-long-enough intervals for conversation and digestion. Individual requests are happily taken, and there is a vegetarian platter entree on the menu.

The intelligent wine list offers over twenty-eight wines by the glass, lots of decent to exceptional California wines, Merlots, French reds, Italian whites and reds, champagnes and sparkling wines, and special bottle selections of the month. Many of the wines are coded and refer to ratings given by *The Wine Spectator,* ranging from good to the highest rating, classic.

Osteria

58 S. Federal Place. 986-5858.

Chef Bruno Pertusina

Lunch:	11 A.M.-5 P.M. Mon.-Sat.
Dinner:	5 P.M.-9 P.M. Mon.-Thurs.; 5 P.M.-10 P.M. Fri.-Sat.
Features:	Closed Sunday. Beer/wine. Smoke-free. Patio.
Price:	Budget/Inexpensive. Major credit cards.
Cuisine:	Italian.

A remodeled old federal building sets the tone for this light, bright space that is now an Italian restaurant, deli, bakery, and take-out. Owner Lino Pertusina (he also owns The Palace restaurant) has cheered up the former dull interior with pale pink plaster walls, lots of potted geraniums, rosy saltillo floor tiles, ash-colored wood floors, French doors, skylights, a fireplace, flagstone patio under lovely cottonwood trees, true-divided casement windows, attractive ironwork, and an upstairs private dining room with another fireplace. Even the bold paintings of pears, pomegranates,and tomatoes are uplifting.

Cases full of salads, cheeses, prosciutto, and desserts start to whet your appetite before you sit down. There are dozens of house-made loaves of *Ciabatta,* a flattish, chewy, thick–crusted, olive oil-based Italian bread stuffed in wooden tubs on top of the cases for taking home as soon as they leave the ovens. This bread is excellent and I prefer it over the too-doughy *panini* that is presented in a basket for the table. Thankfully, three of the sandwiches use their Ciabatta. The *Medallion of Pork Milanese Sandwich* stuffed with red, sweet peppers, avocado, and two good slices of pork with great Milanese sauce was hard to handle, but wanting every bite, not impossible.

A state-of-the-art pasta machine insures fresh pasta for the four pasta dishes that appear on the menu everyday. The *Mushroom and Barley Soup* is almost faultless but the kitchen has a tendency to be heavy-handed with salt—a problem that will hopefully be corrected. Specials of the day might be *Striped Bass* with onion, tomato, and arugula relish or a *Veal Rollatini*—veal roast rolled with prosciutto and fresh spinach—tarragon potatoes and roasted vegetables on the side. A really good vinaigrette using honey and raspberry vinegar dresses a fresh salad of baby greens.

Desserts include a killer *Lemon Meringue Pie*—but the slice is as thin as a knife blade and you'll crave more.

Osteria offers eleven micro-brews with sly names like *Naked Aspen* made with raspberries, wheat, and honey, *Flying Doggie Ale,* which won a gold medal at the 10th Great American Beer Festival, and *Great Divide,* a whitewater wheat ale that won a silver medal at the same festival in 1994. There's seven other beers and a short wine list.

The deli menu is anything but short: nine meats, twelve cheeses, six salads, five vegetable antipastis, and the two house-made breads—all for take-out. If you're waiting for a deli order, pick up some Fini pasta or Sansiro Panetone to go with it. The food and service can be a bit jagged, but Osteria is definitely a place to watch.

The Palace

142 W. Palace Avenue. 982-9891.

Chef Marco Aragone

Lunch:	11:30 A.M.-4 P.M. Mon-Sat.
Limited	
Lunch Menu:	2:30 P.M.-4 P.M. Mon-Sat
Dinner:	5:45 P.M.-10 P.M. daily.
Bar:	11:30 A.M.-2 A.M. Mon-Sat & 5 P.M.-midnight on Sun.
Features:	Piano bar. Full bar. Smoking/non-smoking.
	Cigar friendly in bar. Patio. [Historical]
Price:	Moderate/Expensive. Major credit cards.
Cuisine:	Italian/Continental. (Menus change seasonally.)

*O*nce a gambling hall and house of ill-repute in the 1800s, this site now houses an Italian dinner house complete with red leather booths and white linen table napkins folded into fancy shapes—you know, continental style. In the summer lunch and dinner is served on the tree-covered patio. Luncheons are light and breezy with six homemade pastas, sandwiches, entrees, and five different salads.

The dinner menu features eight appetizers, a good *Caesar Salad* prepared table-side, entrees like *Roasted Glazed Duckling Frangelico* with Hazelnut sauce, wild rice, and red cabbage; or *Veal Scallopine Saltimbocca* with Fontina cheese, sage, prosciutto, polenta, and Marsala wine sauce, and a variety of pastas.

An old-fashioned, four-tiered dessert cart is wheeled up to your table displaying cakes, tortes, and assorted Italian sweets. There's something very comforting about a place like The Palace—somehow you know that everything will turn out just fine.

Plus: The Palace's long-time bartender, Alfonso Alderette, still makes a mean martini.

Paul's

✪

72 West Marcy Street. 982-8738.

Lunch:	11:30 A.M.-2:15 P.M. Mon.-Sat.
Dinner:	5:30 P.M.-9 P.M. Sun.-Thurs.; 6 P.M.-10 P.M. Fri. & Sat.
Features:	Beer/wine. Smoke-free.
Price:	Moderate/Expensive. Major credit cards.
Cuisine:	American/Italian.

Chef and owner Paul Hunsicker has created a small, intimate niche-of-a-restaurant on one of Santa Fe's most charming old streets. By day lunches are above and beyond ordinary fare.

Order a fresh *Caesar* or *Nicoise salad* or *Dill Salmon Cakes* with chipotle lime aioli. There are sandwiches of course but with special twists like *Fresh "Ahi" Tuna* or *Roasted Fresh Turkey Breast* with smoked Gouda.

At night Paul's takes on a more romantic, bistro-like glow and calls for a glass of Tuscany's *Rosso Di Altesino* to go with the *Red Chile Duck Wontons* (with soy-ginger cream) appetizer. Entrees like the *Pumpkin Bread* with piñons, corn, squash and green chile, served with red chile sauce, queso blanco and caramelized apples and the *Baked Salmon* in pecan-herb crust with sorrel sauce have become favorites with the locals.

Save room for Paul's winning *Chocolate Ganache,* marbled with imported white and bittersweet chocolates in a pecan crust to share with your table.

Piñon Grill

100 Sandoval Street. (Enter through the Hilton or entrance on West San Francisco Street.) 988-2811.

Chef Cliff Tanouye

Dinner:	5 P.M.-10 P.M. daily.
Features:	Full bar. Smoke-free. [Historical]
Price:	Moderate/Expensive. Major credit cards.
Cuisine:	American.

*T*his hotel eatery offers what the management calls "New Western Cuisine" and is housed in the 350-year-old Ortiz adobe hacienda. The atmosphere is casual American Steakhouse. All the beef served at the Piñon Grill is Certified Hereford Beef (CHB)—these cattle are corn fed for a minimum of four months and each cut is dry aged for twenty-one days, ensuring tender, juicy, flavorful steaks.

The 10-ounce *New York Strip* is cooked perfectly pink (medium) and is, as promised, tender and juicy. Steaks are grilled with fancy woods like pecan and sassafras along with mesquite; the meat is pre-seasoned with their own special rub, and then served with gravy boats of molasses steak sauce and green chile cream sauce on the side. The green chile cream sauce is a strange pairing with steak—I thought it would be great as a soup. But the molasses sauce is delicious and works well with the meat.

Their five-hour, *Slow-roasted Prime Rib* can be ordered "chile-seared"—crusted with their own chile rub or regular. The cuts are generous and if you eat dinner before 6:45 P.M. the restaurant gives a discount on the prime rib.

If meat isn't your cup of tea, the menu offers an herb-marinated rotisserie chicken, grilled salmon or swordfish, and a fire-grilled and roasted vegetable platter. The *Grilled Portobello Mushrooms* served with aioli is one of the best starters—actually big enough for two. And there are three salads—field greens, wilted spinach, and Caesar that you can make into entrees by adding shrimp, steak, chicken, or lamb. All in all, you'll be satisfied if you stick to the steaks and prime rib.

Plaza Restaurant

54 Lincoln Avenue. 982-1664.

Breakfast/	
Lunch/Dinner:	7 A.M.-10 P.M. Mon.-Sat.; 8 A.M.-10 P.M. Sun.
Features:	Beer/wine with meals only. Smoking/non-smoking. [Historical]
Price:	Inexpensive/Moderate. Visa/MasterCard.
Cuisine:	American, Greek, New Mexican.

Situated right smack-dab on the west side of the Plaza, this cafe has been here forever, or so it seems. It remains an early morning favorite for artists and dealers during Santa Fe's Indian Market.

Over the years, faithful locals like New Mexico's renowned artist William (Bill) Lumpkins and his wife Norma have always headed for the the Plaza Cafe for an early "Indian Market" breakfast. It's a great place to watch the folks sitting on the plaza benches, or to greet long-time friends over a sandwich and a cup of coffee. The menu is eclectic with everything from New Mexican specials to Greek dishes to American burgers.

This place is strictly family. Even though the high influx of tourists have made it hard to get into, do like the locals do—try the 7 A.M. crowd.

Roque's Carnitas ✪

Outdoor cart located at Southeastern corner of the plaza at Palace and Washington Streets.

Lunch:	All day April through October.
Price:	Inexpensive. No credit cards.
Cuisine:	Mexican.

Sooner or later the rich, the poor, the famous, the unknown, the great, the small, all queue-up on the sidewalk by Roque's cart for a hand-held lunch.

Watch Roque (rhymes with Monet) and partner Mona vigorously stir and

mix chiles and onions with marinated steak strips on a fire-hot grill, pile a generous portion of the savory mixture onto a hot, thick, flour tortilla, top it off with Mona's special salsa, and wrap it up in foil. The end result is more like what many of us think are fajitas rather than carnitas. But who cares—it's very tasty, inexpensive, and satisfying.

Before you leave the cart, carnitas in hand, grab plenty of napkins to catch the drips and head for a park bench in the plaza to chow-down. Soft drinks and lemonade are also available.

San Francisco Street Bar & Grill

114 W. San Francisco. 982-2044.

Lunch/Dinner: **11 A.M.-11 P.M. daily.**
Features: **Full bar. Smoke-free.**
Price: **Inexpensive. Visa/MasterCard.**
Cuisine: **American/New Mexican.**

*L*ocated smack-dab in the middle of the Plaza Mercado shopping mall—near the plaza—famished shoppers drop in at this convienient place to get a burger served with pretty good fries.

It's open late every night 'til 11 P.M. and not too many places are open that late in Santa Fe. They also have a courtyard patio that faces Water Street—open May through September from 11 A.M. until late afternoon.

Santacafé

✪ ✪ ✪

231 Washington Avenue. 984-1788.

Lunch:	11:30 A.M.-2 P.M. **Mon-Fri.**
Dinner:	6 P.M.-10 P.M. **daily. Summer:** 5:30 P.M.-10 P.M.
Features:	**Full bar. Patio. Smoke-free dining rooms.**
	Smoking permitted in bar and patio. Free parking lot.
	[Historical]
Price:	**Moderate/Expensive. Visa/MasterCard.**
Cuisine:	**Modern American. (Menu changes seasonally.)**

Santacafé is housed in the one of the finest examples of Placita style architecture remaining in Sante Fe—thanks to Padre Gallegos, who bought the house in 1857 and repaired and enlarged it during his lifetime. Gallegos was a priest who was later defrocked by Bishop Lamy. He went on to become a well-known politician and then, Superintendent of Indian Affairs, in 1868.

The southwest corner of his house is now Santacafé, hidden from the street and marked only by an understated sign that barely announces the restaurant's presence. Walking to the entrance of Santacafé means passing through the courtyard garden-patio that is unquestionably a gorgeous place to eat in warm months.

Immediately inside there is an L-shaped bar and waiting area. Walk to the left and you'll come across a piece of thick plexiglass embedded in the floor covering an opening that is an old excavated well. Vertigo sufferers may want to step around it. To the right are four, very minimal, intimate dining rooms, each with its own fireplace. Quiet white dominates: stark blank walls (some are two-feet thick), bleached antlers above each fireplace, starched table linens, and simple, shuttered white-paned windows all lend a zen-like appeal to the place and keeps the spare ambience at full tilt.

Even though the menu has seen some recent changes, and owners Judy Ebbinghaus and Bobby Morean stress modern American cuisine—Santacafé's kitchen keeps an ingenious menu filled with American, Asian, and Southwestern flavors.

High praise and fame for Santacafé has come from famous food critics, and national publications like *Conde-Nast Traveler, Bon Appetit, Gourmet* magazine, and the *New York Times.* Celebrities are known to reserve weeks in advance

Coriander Crusted Ahi Tuna with Shaved Fennel Salad and Chile-Cilantro Vinaigrette

Ingredients for the Ahi Tuna and Crust:

> *#1 Grade Ahi Tuna cut into 1 x 1 x 4 inch pieces. Triangular shape works well.*
> 1/2   *cup Coriander seed, untoasted*
> 1   *tablespoon white peppercorns*
> 1/2   *tablespoon salt*

Method:

Using a coffee/spice grinder, coarse-grind the coriander seeds and peppercorns. Mix ground coriander, peppercorn, and salt. Coat each piece of Ahi Tuna completely. Set aside. Pre-heat a non-stick pan to medium-high flame. Spray pan or lightly rub with olive oil. Sear each side very rare or cook to your preference. (Chef's note: With #1 Ahi, it would be a shame to cook it more than rare. Let stand for 30 minutes before slicing.)

Ingredients for the Chile-Cilantro Vinaigrette:

> 5   *Serrano peppers, roasted and peeled*
> 1/2   *bunch cilantro, de-stemmed*
> 1/2   *cup honey*
> 3   *cups light oil*
> 1/2   *cup rice vinegar*
> *Salt and pepper to taste*

Method:

Blend peppers with cilantro, honey, and vinegar. Add oil and salt and pepper. Mix together.

Ingredients for the finish:

> *shaved fennel*
> *fresh, chopped cilantro*
> *chile oil*
> *sliced scallions*
> *daikon sprouts (if available)*

Serving instructions:

Toss shaved fennel with the vinaigrette and more fresh-chopped cilantro. Place a mound of this mixture in the middle of the plate. Surround the salad with 3 slices of the seared tuna. Garnish plate with more vinaigrette and chile oil in a zig-zag pattern. Sprinkle with sliced scallions and daikon sprouts. Place potato crisps, fried potatoes or a large potato chip on top of the salad.

Yield: 4 servings

which is what you should do, too.

It is said that you can tell a good restaurant by its bread; and if it's good then you might as well settle in for a terrific meal. Well, the bread here is good. Chile pepper brioche along with house-made, crispy crackers arrive at your table in no time—so start ordering.

Santacafé changes its menu seasonally and the menus reflect New Mexico's wonderful, organic produce and natural meats that are being used in more and more upscale Santa Fe restaurants. You must start your meal with their famous *Shrimp Dumplings* in spicy sauce. The *Crispy Calamari* with soy-lime dipping sauce is always a treat and *Hearts of Romaine Caesar Salad* with chile brioche croutons wouldn't be a bad choice, either. And don't pass up the elegant and savory *Grilled Corn Vichyssoise*.

Main courses might include their tried-and-true *Cornmeal Crusted Ruby Red Trout* with roasted corn and black bean ragout; or *Angel Hair Pasta* with mussels, shrimp, arugula and house-smoked tomato sauce. I couldn't help ordering one of their signature dishes that was pictured on the cover of the September, 1994, *Bon Appetit*—the *Grilled Filet Mignon* with roasted garlic-green chile mashed potatoes. It didn't fail.

The dessert menu offers extravagant choices so you won't be able to resist all of them. Maybe it's time to indulge in the *Warm Chocolate Upside-down Cake* or their *Classic Creme Brulee*.

The Shed

---

113 1/2 E. Palace Avenue. 982-9030.

Lunch:	11 A.M.-2:30 P.M. Mon-Sat.
Dinner:	5:30 P.M.-9 P.M. Wed.-Sat.
Features:	Beer/Wine. Smoke-free. Patio. [Historical]
Price:	Inexpensive. No credit cards.
Cuisine:	New Mexican.

Some locals say this is the best Native New Mexican cooking in Santa Fe and, well, it *is* a local institution. The Shed is housed in a seventeenth-century hacienda so you get the feeling of what it was like to live in an old adobe.

The Shed has been around since 1954 and continues to turn out those great— perhaps, even legendary, stacked, red or green chile enchiladas using blue corn tortillas. There's also posole, burritos, beans, and house-made desserts. The delicious chile is made every morning at their sister restaurant, La Choza, and brought over in big containers.

Plus: If you want to avoid the tourist crowds and long lines during the summer, drive over to The Shed's offspring, La Choza, located off Cerrillos Road near St. Francis Boulevard, where you can stretch out and get the same great, classic food at low prices.

The Staab House at La Posada

330 E. Palace Avenue. 986-0000.

Breakfast: 7 A.M.-11 A.M. daily.
Lunch: 11:30 A.M.-2 P.M. daily.
Dinner: 6 P.M.-10 P.M. daily.
Features: Full bar. Smoking/nonsmoking. Patio.
     Free parking lot. [Historical]
Price: Moderate/Expensive. Major credit cards.
Cuisine: American/Mediterranean/New Mexican.

The history and architecture of The Staab House may be more exciting than the food. The restaurant bears the name of one of its many land owners, immigrant Abraham Staab, a prominent Jewish mercantile businessman who built a mansion for his German bride, Julia Schuster Staab, around 1876. He chose to build in the French Second Empire style. Therefore all the building materials were brought to Santa Fe by steamer and wagon train from the east. Mahogany, marble, and brick were used to construct a building that was quite different from the traditional styles Santa Feans were used to.

By 1936, several owners and additions later, R.H. and Eulalia Nason purchased the residence that now had seventeenth-century adobe structures incorporated into the original building. The Nasons fancied the Pueblo Revival movement—so a series of casitas were built on the site using local clay and straw and the buildings became "La Posada" meaning inn, lodging, or resting place.

The entire Second Empire and Victorian features of the Staab house were gradually taken over by the Pueblo-style architecture and was eventually developed by the Nasons into a serious, major resort hotel that catered to a summer art school at the inn. And the visiting artists and art students helped make Santa Fe a flourishing art colony, as it remains today.

Newer casita additions have been built, making the La Posada one of the more desirable hotels to stay at in Santa Fe. The six acres of grounds offer visitors and locals a beautiful park-like setting with meandering walks, a white gazebo, a glorious flagstone patio, pots and pots of red geraniums in the summer surrounding the pool, and a three-tiered water fountain set in the dining area that bubbles and cools in the summer.

The Stabb House kitchen needs to concentrate on updating the quality and consistency of their food and service staff. An eating experince here can be iffy and service is definitely not up-to-snuff. Too bad, because the setting is marvelous. If you're staying at the hotel you can get a Mediterranean buffet lunch Monday through Friday in the dining room or out on the patio—and not really be disappointed.

A great thing about La Posada is the bar. It consists of three rooms. The first room is dark and has a burnished wood bar just right for a drink before dinner. The next two rooms have old fashioned windows covered in lace curtains, working fireplaces, Victorian-style tables, wing chairs and setees, crystal chandeliers, a piano (for romantic serenades), and a set of French doors that exit to an elevated, brick-floored deck for outside drinks in warm weather.

In the winter, though, there's nothing more cozy than ordering some hot buttered rums, sitting close to one of the fires, and maybe playing a hand of poker with friends and drifting back in time while the world outside turns white.

Tia Sophia's

✪

210 W. San Francisco Street. 983-9880.

Breakfast:	7 A.M.-11 A.M. Mon.-Sat.
Lunch:	11 A.M.-2 P.M. Mon.-Sat.
Features:	No alcohol. Smoking/non-smoking.
Price:	Budget/Inexpensive. Visa/MasterCard/Traveler's checks.
Cuisine:	New Mexican.

This is such a local favorite you may have a short wait to get seated at one of the old wooden booths or a table. Numbers are handed out in order of your appearance. And in the cold months, everyone huddles inside the tiny foyer. Lawyers in suits, their clients, and just about everybody else in town shows up sooner or later for the green chile stew (known to cure the common cold), and enormous breakfast burritos stuffed with bacon, potatoes, chile, and cheese (they say they were invented here).

Breakfast specials Monday through Saturday are great bargains and on Saturday you can get the burrito with Tia Sophia's own hot and spicy chorizo (sausage). Besides the specials, there are classic Huevos Rancheros, omelets, eggs, cheese enchiladas, egg, sausage, bacon, or ham rolls, chile relleno, bowls of red or green chile, pancakes, cereals, sides of breakfast meats, and posole.

Lunch specials Monday through Saturday also offer great bargains. The Thursday special, *Carne Avocado Burrito* with chile and cheese, rice, beans, and a basket of hard-to-match sopaipillas to cool down the mouth is a mere $6.25. By the way, their sopaipillas are heavenly—all puffy and flaky—ask for butter and honey to go-with.

Enchiladas, cheese or meat, abound and there are chile rellenos, tamales, tostadas, and an *Atrisco Plate* consisting of chile stew, cheese enchilada, beans, and posole. This plate's a good choice for sampling a lot of New Mexican dishes. You can also get hamburgers, fries, chef's salad, guacamole salad, tuna sandwich in pita, and *Sophia's Sandwich*—ham and melted cheese with lettuce, tomato, avocado, and salsa served open-faced on a flour tortilla.

There's a vegetarian combo of beans and rice and, of course, you can order the chile vegetarian. If you order coffee or iced tea, refills are on the house. Be aware of friendly warnings on both menus: "Not responsible for too hot chile" and "Positively no exchanges on meals if not ordered as vegetarian."

Service is no-nonsense fast and efficient. Tia Sophia's is definitely a must for New Mexican authenticity.

Woolworth's (F.W. Woolworth)

58 E. San Francisco Street. 982-1062

Hours: 8:30 A.M.-8 P.M. Mon.-Fri.; 9 A.M.-7 P.M. Sat.;
              10 A.M.-6 P.M. Sun.
Features: No alcohol. Free parking lot. [Historical]
Price: Inexpensive. Major credit cards.
Cuisine: American/New Mexican.

*O*ne of the last hold-outs of *old* Santa Fe, Woolworth's sits tenuously facing the plaza—you might say, even defiantly, opposing the modernization of plaza real estate that has created so many tourist spots.

It is said that the *Frito Pie* was invented here by Teresa Hernandez back in the 50s. If you've never experienced a Frito pie, you must have one here at its birthplace. Walk over to the deco-style, formica-topped, Blue Plate lunch counter and order a giant-sized Frito pie in, or the regular-sized one to-go. The pie is a somewhat messy, layered combination of corn chips, three-alarm red chile, jalapeños, and chopped onions for the full effect. Plenty of napkins, a cold drink, and a brave tummy are necessary.

Woolworth's brings back all the nostalgia you can handle—so stay awhile and wander. Locals still come here to shop for all those little sundry items like pots and pans, sewing supplies, and good cotton socks.

Bistro 315

315 Old Santa Fe Trail. 986-9190.

Lunch:	11:30 A.M.-2 P.M. daily.
Dinner:	6 P.M.-9 P.M. daily.
Features:	Beer/Wine. Smoke-free inside. Patio.
Price:	Moderate. Major credit cards.
Cuisine:	French Bistro. (Menu changes daily.)

"*T*wo guys and a bistro!" The two guys are hard-working owners, Matt Yohalem and Jack Shaab, who have cleverly created an instantly-popular eatery. Wedged into its site on Old Santa Fe Trail, the bistro's front, tent-covered patio saves it from becoming claustrophobic. This place is so tiny, that specials might be announced to all the diners at once. And I suspect the chef can overhear diners' remarks about his cooking from the kitchen. In true bistro style, the menu changes every day and is presented on chalkboards posted around the dining areas, and the tables sport white linen covered with white butcher paper.

The bread is good, crusty and chewy. They serve the town's favorite *Fano's Rustic Loaf,* delivered to them bakery-fresh every morning. The menu is seasonal and there are usually eight to ten entrees offered at lunch and dinner. The kitchen can be heavy on butter and cream, so be careful about ordering if you're counting fat grams. The daily differences in the menus are slight: a grilled fish and/or steak entree could be added to the dinner menu.

Soup might be a smokey, garlicy, grilled tomato with a tiny tangle of carmelized leeks floating on top. There are always one or two salads, and some interesting first courses or side orders such as *Duck Liver Mousse con Crostini* or *Braised Endive & Potato Cake.*

Some samples of the entrees are: *Grilled Smoked Chicken, Steak with Pomme Frites* that are crispy and addictive, *Seafood Papiotte,* or *Quail and Mushroom Risotto,* and their incredible stuffed *Portobello Mushrooms.* The braised, carmelized baby vegetables served with many of the entrees are superb. A simple roast chicken with braised red cabbage and veal scallopinni are are the lighter side. If cassoulet is offered, it's a good choice.

If you can possibly find room, order at least one of their desserts. The best one so far is the *tarte tartin* served warm with a proper dollop of *creme fraiche.*

Bistro 315 may be small but the the food is big with flavor. You might guess that reservations are a must.

Guadalupe Cafe

✪

422 Old Santa Fe Trail. 982-9762.

Breakfast:	7 A.M.-11 A.M Tues.-Fri.; 8 A.M.-2 P.M. Sat. & Sun.
Lunch:	11 A.M.-2 P.M. Tues.-Sat.
Dinner:	5:30 P.M.-10 P.M. Tues.-Sat.
Features:	Beer/wine. Smoke-free. Patio. Free parking lot.
Price:	Inexpensive. Visa/MasterCard.
Cuisine:	New Mexican.

Guadalupe Cafe's new digs are more upscale than their old ones—but nothing much else has changed. They are now housed in a bright, old adobe with several small rooms that give a feeling of intimacy. The floors are wood, and there's a fireplace in the front room as well as one in the kitchen. The cooks laughed when I asked them if they ever fired it up. "No, we would rather have air conditioning." This new space has more sun streaming through the windows and tables are tiled—everything fresh and neat. A pleasant front patio facing Old Santa Fe Trail gets a lot of use in summer.

Still proudly serving their house-made hot red and green chiles, the waitresses will gladly give samples to cautious diners. A note on the menu warns those with unaccustomed palates to sample the chile first. I find their chile just the right hotness—not too much heat so the complex, rich flavors come through.

Guadalupe's breakfasts are guaranteed to satisfy the most demanding lumberjack-type appetite. Get a handle on *Jumbo Burritos, Huevos Rancheros, Stacked Enchiladas, Eggs Benedict* that transcend the ordinary with red or green chile hollandaise (get both—get Christmas), *French Toast* using homemade cinnamon nut bread, and *chile-cheese homefries. Migas* are scrambled eggs with scallions, chile, cheese, and crisp tortilla strips stirred in. The "from scratch" fresh *Buttermilk Raspberry Pancakes* are delectable—with plump, ruby red raspberries imbedded into the tender cakes. *Blue Corn Piñon* comes in a close second.

Lunch and dinner offer consistently great New Mexican fare from several kinds of *enchiladas,* to *chalupas* (corn tortilla baskets nestling chicken, beans, and guacamole with cheese, green chile, salsa, and sour cream on top)—a hefty dish to be sure. Most orders come with excellent *sopapillas*—and there's honey to drizzle on top. No skimping on ingredients here—cheeses are full-bodied Cheddars and Montery Jacks. Blue corn tortillas grace enchilada plates. The *Guadalupe Special Sandwich*—grilled turkey, avocado, Jack cheese with pesto mayonnaise put together on their grilled, homemade bread (wholewheat or sourdough), is out-standing. Lots of eight-ounce burgers like the *Zozobra Burger* with grilled mush-rooms and Swiss cheese are always made right. Try one of their *Stuffed Sopapillas* if you've never had one.

Dinner offers some New Mexican specialties that you can't get at lunch. *Breast of Chicken Relleno* is a chicken breast (instead of a long, green chile) stuffed with Jack and Cheddar cheeses, deep fried and oven-fired with green chile and more cheese. Showing midwest roots with a twist, *Chicken Fried Chicken Steak* and *Turkey Piñon Meatloaf* appear both served with *homemade mashed potatoes*. The nifty *Plato Grande* or build-your-own-combination-plate is a grand idea. This way you can try two of their New Mexican specials (enchilada and burrito) on the same plate. Be warned—*burritos* are big, but even elderly folks who come in for lunch don't blink an eye when the giant ones are set before them.

Desserts sell out quickly—this is no lie—so you may want to put your dessert order in when you order entrees. The decadent house-made *Adobe Pie* and *Heath Bar Pie* are always on the menu. Daily specials and desserts like banana cream pie and entrees of-the-day are posted on a board by the cashier's counter. (Check out the 1907 brass cash register.)

Owner Isabelle Koomoa and her staff are downright friendly, making you feel at home in this unpretentious restaurant that was here long before "nouvelle" came to town.

Old Santa Fe Trail Bookstore & Bistro

613 Old Sant Fe Trail. 988-8878.

Breakfast/ Lunch/Dinner:	**8 A.M.-10 P.M. Mon.-Thurs.; 8 A.M.-11 P.M. Fri. & Sat.; 8 A.M.-5 P.M. Sun.**
Features:	**Full bar. Non-smoking inside. Smoking permitted on patio.**
Price:	**Inexpensive. Major credit cards.**
Cuisine:	**American.**

One of the best things about OSFTB&B is their poetry/book readings and booksignings—a great gift to a community that is fast becoming a literary center.

Plan an evening with local poets—go early, order up a *T.B.A.* (turkey, bacon, and avocado sandwich) or the *P.B.T.* (Portobello, basil, and tomato sandwich) and wash it down with a strong espresso or cappuccino. After the reading, have another coffee (so you can stay up late to gab with the poets) and get a fat slice of fruit pie in the summer or a wedge of layer cake in the winter to go with it.

The bookstore section of this establishment is high quality and it's fun to just browse around, find that book you've been looking for, and later cozy-into one of their cushy seats for a good bistro-style dinner.

The Pink Adobe

⭐

406 Old Santa Fe Trail. 983-7712.

Lunch:	**11:30 A.M.-2 P.M. Mon.-Fri.**
Dinner:	**5:30 P.M.-10 P.M. daily.**
Bar hours:	**11:30 A.M.-midnight daily.**
Features:	**Full bar. Smoke-free. Smoking in bar permitted.**
	Free parking lot. Art. [Historical]
Price:	**Moderate. Major credit cards.**
Cuisine:	**American/Creole/New Mexican.**

*L*ocals and those in the know affectionately refer to Rosalea Murphy's eatery as "The Pink." Back in the 40s, the original Pink seated about thirty people. Today, the expanded Pink is housed in a 300-year-old former military barracks with thirty-six-inch thick walls, six fireplaces, and pink stucco exterior—what else? Art, handmade pottery, and murals abound here. In fact, once a year, Ms. Murphy puts on a self-portrait show for local artists at the Pink with prizes, awards, foods, and wines to celebrate the art and participating artists.

Artists, famous and not-so-famous, have always hung out at The Pink, especially in the Dragon Room Bar. This bar is crammed with locals and visitors every night of the week during the summer. With standing room only, the lure of tradition, celebrity watching, and free, fresh-popped popcorn make this watering hole one of the most popular in Santa Fe. Try the *Creole Mary*—a Bloody Mary made with Stoli and a garden-sink skewer of celery, olives, and pickled okra!

Lunch in the Dragon Room is real fine and there's a fireplace to take off the winter chill while you wait for the Pink's renowned *Gypsy Stew,* a unique blend of chicken, garlic, green chiles, sherry, and cheese. If you miss Rosalea's terrific *Green*

Chile Stew, it's available at some markets in their freezer section.

Murphy came to Santa Fe from New Orleans with her Creole-Cajun food sensibilities, combined them with her new-found knowledge of New Mexican food, and developed some rather delicious, eclectic recipes: The ever-popular *Steak Dunigan* (New York cut sirloin smothered with green chile sauce and sauteed mushrooms and named after Rosalea's friend, Pat Dunigan, who asked for green chiles on his steak over thirty years ago) is one of the signature dishes.

The *French Apple Pie* remains one of the best and most favored desserts on the menu. What makes this pie so good? Probably the lard that is used to make the delectable pastry, and its filling chock-full of apples, nuts, and raisins. It's served up warm with a hot brandy sauce ladeled over the top. Makes you feel like it's Christmas Eve every time you have it.

The main building across the driveway from the Dragon Room holds four dining rooms, all different. The intimate Pit, a tiny room with only four tables, has a fireplace for all to enjoy; the Blue Room, the romantic Alcove Room, and the New Room make up the other three, all equally inviting.

If you can't get along at home without Rosalea's dishes, she has written two cookbooks, *The Pink Adobe* and *In The Pink,* so you can prepare them in your own kitchen. (I make *Gypsy Stew* at home quite often. Always a hit. Maybe it's the bottle of sherry that goes into it? The Pink's equally popular *Chicken Hash in Grits Ring* recipe appears on page 76.)

The Pink Adobe's Signature Dish

Chicken Hash in Grits Ring

Ingredients for grits ring:

4	cups water
1	teaspoon salt
1	cup quick-cooking grits
3	tablespoons butter
3	eggs, separated
1/4	cup shredded Cheddar cheese

Ingredients for chicken hash:

1/2	cup (1 cube) butter
1/4	cup chopped onion
1/2	cup chopped celery
3	tablespoons flour
1-1/2	cups warm chicken broth
2	tablespoons heavy cream
2	tablespoons Madeira wine
1	teaspoon salt
1/4	teaspoon pepper
1/4	cayenne
3	cups cooked and diced chicken
1-1/2	cups peeled and diced cooked potatoes

Method for grits ring:

Preheat oven to 350 degrees. Bring the water and salt to a boil. Stir in the grits and cook until thickened. (Quick-cooking grits take about 5 minutes.) Remove from heat. Add the butter, cover, and let stand until cool. In a small bowl, beat the egg yolks. In another bowl, beat the egg whites until very stiff. Stir the egg yolks and cheese into the grits mixture. Fold in the beaten egg whites. Generously grease a 10-inch ring mold. Put the grits into the mold and place the mold in a baking pan containing 1 inch of water. Bake for 1 hour (cooking time may vary, depending on your oven), until the top is golden brown. Cool for 10 to 15 minutes before removing from mold. To unmold grits ring, run a silver knife around the sides of the mold to loosen. Invert onto a large platter.

Method for chicken hash:

Melt the butter in a heavy saucepan. Lightly sauté the onion and celery for a few minutes. Stir in the flour and cook over medium heat for 2 minutes. Slowly pour in the chicken broth and stir until thickened. Stir in the cream and Madeira. If sauce is too thick, add a little more cream. Add seasonings and gently stir in chicken and potatoes. Heat through. Pour the chicken hash into center of the unmolded grits ring. Serve immediately.

Yield: 6 servings

(Reprinted with permission from *In the Pink,* by Doubleday, a division of Bantam Doubleday Dell Publishing Group, Inc., New York.)

Upper Crust Pizza

329 Old Santa Fe Trail. 983-4140.

Lunch/Dinner: 11 A.M.-11 P.M. daily.
Features: Beer/wine. Smoking/nonsmoking. Patio.
                  [Historical]
Price: Budget/Inexpensive. Major credit cards.
Cuisine: Italian.

*U*pper Crust Pizza announces on a board near the order counter that they use only *real* cheese, meats, and vegetables. If the word "real" is used to describe foods in the United States, FDA stamped-approved language says it is the real thing. This important bit of information might change the way you see pizza parlors from now on or, for that matter, any food establishment you may question. Always ask the management if they use real stuff. There are plenty of restaurants that use phony food deceptions to cut costs. *But not here.*

Part of Upper Crust's claim to fame is that they are next door to the oldest continuously used church in the United States—dating back to Santa Fe's founding in 1610. And they inhabit the oldest building in the United States. Another is their homemade whole wheat pizza crusts. Everything here is simple and easy. Get in line, order, sit down, and a wait person will deliver the goods while shouting out your name.

The lunchtime crowd shows off Santa Fe's cultural diversity: families, suits, the T-shirt crowd, tennies, Anglos, Hispanics, Native Americans, and tourists.

One reason for Upper Crust's eternal popularity is the $2.99 lunch special: a slice (sorry, no whole wheat, but the regular crust is plenty fine) with choice of one topping, a drink, and a fair-to-middling mixed green salad with choice of Blue Cheese, Ranch, Thousand Island, or oil and vinegar dressings. Pizza is also available in 10-inch and 15-inch pies, and you can add over twenty toppings or choose the specialty pizzas like the *Grecian Gourmet* with Feta cheese, black olives, bell peppers, mushrooms, and garlic.

House specialties include an intriguing *Sausage Roll:* a spicy Italian sausage covered in their rich tomato sauce, chile, and onion topped with Mozzarella cheese and blanketed in pizza dough. So if you like your crusts thin and crisp with lots of real stuff on top, then this is the right place.

Downtown Subscription

376 Garcia Street. 983-3085.

Breakfast/	
Lunch:	7:30 A.M.-7 P.M. Mon.-Thurs. & 7:30 A.M.-9 P.M. Fri. & Sat.
Features:	No alcohol. Smoke-free. Smoking permitted on the patio.
Price:	Inexpensive. No credit cards.
Cuisine:	American.

*I*t's a newsstand. It's a coffeebar. It's a spot to peruse over 1600 magazine titles and have an espresso, a cappuccino, and a pastry.

Local writers are all here, chatting over coffee about their latest screenplays, novels, or art-book deals.

A large, lovely patio continues to attract a major segment of the coffee-house crowd that likes to enjoy New Mexico's year-round days of sunshine.

El Farol

★

808 Canyon Road. 983-9912.

Lunch:	11 A.M.-6 P.M. daily.
Dinner:	6 P.M. -10 P.M. daily.
Features:	Full bar. Live entertainment every night at 9:30 P.M. Smoking/non-smoking. Patio. Art. [Historical]
Price:	Moderate/Expensive. Major credit cards.
Cuisine:	Spanish.

*B*e rewarded with food, drink, and interesting company at the oldest bar in town. El Farol has long been recognized as the unofficial Canyon Road artists' headquarters (lots of local artists still hang out here). And in the old days, it had the notoriety of being one of the wildest, rowdiest bars this side of the Pecos

River. Rumor has it that thirsty cowhands used to ride their horses right into the low-ceilinged bar! Years later, under the direction of owner David Salazar, El Farol added dining areas and a fine selection of tapas and al la carte entrees to become a tamer and decidedly respectable eating establishment.

The small dining rooms have big round wood tables, plank wood floors (keeping the rustic look intact), and white linens. But ask for a back room away from the music if you're sensitive to sound. (Drop in for the live music and enjoy late night cheek-to-cheek dancing on a postage stamp-sized dance floor and rock around the clock, or simply enjoy alternative Flamenco entertainment.)

There are thirty-five tapas on the dinner menu (fewer on the lunch menu) and newer al la carte entree additions featuring Spanish dishes such as *Paella. Grilled Shrimp, Pasta with Scallops, Garlic Soup, Grilled Lamb Chops, Steaks, Roasted Chicken Breast* with smoky chile sauce. And plenty of vegetarian entrees are also on the menu to suit every taste.

If you're not familiar with tapas, here's the scoop. Tapas are appetizers (and can be a full meal as well) that have been served throughout Spain in bars and restaurants for a long time. Sherrys, cocktails, or other apertifs usually accompany tapas. My favorites at El Farol have always been the *Curried Chicken Salad, Roasted Sweet Peppers* with olives and Feta cheese, deep beer-batter-fried *Calamari* with Romesco Sauce (a spicy, rich tomato sauce), and *Lamb Brochette* with mint sauce. The rich and creamy *Pasta with Piñon and Manchego Cheese* is available as a tapa and dinner entree. I insist you get it. It's fun to come here with a large group, order a lot of tapas, and find your own favorites.

The most delightful thing about El Farol is the dimly lit bar where old murals, painted by early New Mexican artist, Alfred Morang, still exist on the walls. It's said he traded the paintings for drink and food. This western-style bar looks rightly old and decrepit with its wood plank floors and thick adobe walls. Occasional clicks from spurred, dusty cowboy boots can almost make you feel that you're back in the eighteenth-century.

Geronimo

● ❂

724 Canyon Road. 982-1500.

Chefs Kirstin and Steven Jarrett

Brunch:	11:30 A.M.-2:15 P.M. Sun.
Lunch:	11:30 A.M.-2:15 P.M. Tues.-Sat.
Dinner:	6 P.M.-10 P.M. daily.
Features:	Full bar. Smoking/non-smoking sections. Patio. Free parking lot. [Historical]
Price:	Expensive. Major credit cards.
Cuisine:	Southwestern. (Menu changes seasonally.)

*I*t all started when Geronimo Lopez built this adobe home in 1756. After 240 years, there have been additions built on to the original structure. But because this landmark building now enjoys historical status, structural changes are difficult, if not impossible. (The manager told me that a recent installation of a big, pump espresso machine "was a plumbing nightmare.")

A cool, long high-ceilinged portal fronts the main entrance to the historical part of Lopez' home which still has the original beams in place. In summer, tables are set up for under-the-portal dining, delivering cool shade and extensive people watching (you're only a step away from Canyon Road). Once inside, look up. You may wonder why the beams aren't round like all the other adobe beams/ vigas in Santa Fe. Back then, most all the wood for building came from east coast lumber mills—and they produced geometric beams.

Geronimo is a real treat, for the asthetically bound and for the judicious palate. When you enter the original building, the first thing you see is a large fireplace sporting an oversized pair of moose antlers above the mantel. There are gleaming, brass-plated dining table tops, twenty-four inch-thick adobe walls, and the aforementioned beams high overhead. The dining tables are nicely spaced— my favorite table is to the far right as you enter, against the inner wall. This table has banco-padded seating with lots of plump pillows and allows you to face out onto the entire room. The more recent rooms (still over 100-years-old) that were added on in the traditional New Mexican way (usually tacked on as the family got larger) are towards the back but no less attractive.

As you head toward the second dining room which also has a fireplace, thick walls, and brass-topped tables, you might want to step into the small, cozy bar with its antler chandelier and corner fireplace. Sit at one of the seven barstools at the (yes) brass-plated bar, and order an aperitif before dinner. Continue on and to the left, peek out the windows at the intimate, four-table patio complete with a charming fountain and coyote fence for privacy—very popular in summer.

Photo by Jackie Mathey

The restaurant has created menus that complement the historical New Mexican tradition of this adobe. Many of the dishes are infused with New Mexican and Southwest ingredients that, literally, sing with flavor and add a unique and sophisticated quality to foods that we are already familiar with.

For example, at brunch the menu might offer the familiar Caesar salad but with a fresh-lime-twist Caesar dressing, grilled jalapeño, fresh cilantro, Pecorino Romano cheese, and housemade toasted sage croutons. A burger here is the *Smoked Black Angus Rib Eye Burger* with a grilled Anaheim chile-pineapple salsa, and Gruyere cheese served with a side of Ancho chile-dusted shoestring potatoes and housemade ketchup; or the *Smoked Norwegian Salmon* over poached eggs with a red chile hollandaise and thyme panfries (takes the place of ordinary Eggs Benedict). Each reflects the Southwestern theme of this restaurant.

The chile rellenos, found on the brunch, lunch, and sometimes dinner menus are like no other you've ever tasted and are by far my all-time favorite rellenos. The ones I've tried are the *Spicy Chicken Mole Relleno* with jalapeño peach salsa, wild greens, and creme fraiche, and another one was stuffed with crispy red corn, lime-grilled steak and topped with a Chipotle chile puree, tomatillo salsa, and creme fraiche. What makes them soooo good is the crunchy red chile crust that envelopes the long, slender green chile—never soggy. Another interesting brunch item is the *Tequila Poached Eggs* with Black Forest Ham and Gruyere cheese on a croissant with Bernaise sauce.

Dinners are splendid with dishes that have lots of New Mexican and French influences: *Mesquite Grilled Three Peppercorn Filet of Beef* with roasted red and green chile scalloped potatoes and a Roquefort-Madeira sauce; or the *Housemade Ravioli* stuffed with lime grilled bay shrimp, montrachet, and grilled summer vegetables with a smoked tomato-chipotle chile cream will keep you smiling.

There are always a lot of choices on the menus and even though the decisions can be difficult, when it comes to dessert the choice is easy—go for the *Mocha Pot de Creme*—chocolate to live for.

Tibet Cafe

403 Canyon Road. 989-8466.

Breakfast:	8 A.M.-11:30 A.M.
Lunch:	11:30 A.M.-2:30 P.M. daily.
Afternoon menu:	2:30 P.M.-6 P.M. daily.
Dinner:	6 P.M.-9 P.M. daily.
Features:	Beer/wine. Smoke free. Patio. Free parking lot.
Price:	Inexpensive/Moderate. Visa/MasterCard.
Cuisine:	Tibetan. (Menu changes seasonally.)

When Tibet lost her freedom in 1959, a migration of Tibetan people flowed into parts of India and the United States. Since Tibet is a country located at an altitude of over 10,000 feet, it makes sense that some of those who immigrated to America would seek out higher ground. Santa Fe stands at 7000 feet—perhaps a paltry height compared to Tibet's, but nevertheless high enough for many Tibetans to feel at home.

Two energetic young men from Tibet, Chophel Phuntsok and Dawa Tsering, opened the Tibet Cafe in the summer of 1995. Phunstok is the chef and co-owner with Tsering, and the two basically run the entire operation.

Simple wood doors and a gauzy, white scarf blessed by the Dalai Lama and wrapped around the doorknobs mark the entrance to the cafe, that opens into a small adobe room with brick floors and a small kiva fireplace in the corner. On the mantel are two photographs of the Dalai Lama placed beside a Tibetan bell and cup. There are Tibetan masks and fabric thankas on the wall and another white prayer shawl wrapped around an interior door knob.

There is a big misconception that Tibetans are vegetarians. I remember a hilarious story about the Dalai Lama and his entourage at the time of their visit to Ojai, California, in the early 80s. The food brigade scrambled to get together all the finest produce they could gather for a veggie feast. Somehow the word leaked down through the ranks that the Dalai Lama loved spaghetti and meatballs! Chagrined but not shaken, the feast-makers quickly changed the menu, much to the delight of the visiting Tibetans. And a valuable piece of historical information was learned about the food of Tibet: vegetarian cuisine is almost impossible in their homeland climate. At an altitude with a very short growing season, little food for domesticated animals, few varieties of produce, reduced oxygen, and rugged winters—Tibet's cuisine reflects these conditions.

Due to the many years of trade relations with India, China, and Nepal, Tibet's food is laced with spices from these countries: cumin, ginger, cinnamon, tumeric, coriander, fenugreek and sesame seeds. Yak meat and butter, seasonal-stream fish, barley, noodles, tea, and simple vegetables such as spinach and pickled cucumbers or radishes have served as traditional fare for many years in Tibet. Therefore, the menu at the Tibet Cafe uses chicken, ground beef, salmon and trout, and lamb—all easily available in New Mexico. Tibetan cuisine also includes cilantro, garlic, and chiles—ingredients that are used in cooking around the world. Add yogurt, and basmati rice and before you can say *"Tashi Delek"* you have an updated version of Tibetan cuisine sitting on your plate.

Enough vegetable-only dishes are here to make even the most strict vegetarians bliss-out.

Appetizers, lunch and dinner entrees feature one of the most traditional Tibetan dishes, *momo. Momo* is a steamed or pan-seared dumpling that is stuffed with ground beef and is served here at dinner with a fire-roasted fenugreek seed tomato sauce (remember the spaghetti and meatballs?) or mustard sesame sauce and sesame cucumber salad. There is also a Garden momo—*Tsel-Mo*— that is stuffed with cabbage, spinach, and bok choy served with the tomato sauce and salad. *Jha-Sha-Kha-Tsa* (Chicken Chile) is an appetizer using pieces of chicken sauteed with red onions, garlic, and bell pepper; another is *Sha-Kha-Tsa,* roasted beef marinated in leeks, ginger, garlic, and cumin.

Dinners are surprisingly diverse: *Luc-Sha,* Pala's Tibetan lamb curry marinated in red wine, ginger, garlic, rosemary, and bay leaves with yogurt, and a scallion-steamed roll or *Ser-Nya,* baked salmon marinated in balsamic vinegar, basil, tarragon, cumin, and cayenne, also with a scallion-steamed roll or *Dey-Tsel,* Tibetan curry with tofu, broccoli, cauliflower, and bok choy on Basmati rice.

There are side orders of Basmati rice (with the flavor and aroma of popcorn),

Amala's tomato sauce (not ordinary), and a fresh garden salad.

Highly recommended is the *Eastern Tibet Tea* (something like the familiar Yogi Tea that's been in our markets for a long time) and a Tibetan beer to go with the curry. In Tibet they add a couple of dollops of Yak butter to the tea to get everyone through the winter.

Two desserts are offered, *Tibetan Yogurt* with fruit and honey and a *Chocolate Torte*. By the way, what does *Tashi Delek* mean? "May good and healthy things happen to you!"—a phrase that is printed on the back of the menus. This I can assure you, Tibet Cafe's food is healthy and energizing—what else, with the Dalai Lama presiding over all?

Trixie's Cafe

802 Canyon Road. 983-5040.

Breakfast/	
Lunch:	8 A.M.-5 P.M. daily.
Features:	Beer/wine. Smoke-free. Patio. Art. [Historical]
Price:	Budget. No credit cards.
Cuisine:	American

*T*he new kids on the block may have famous parents, but celebrity gawkers should put this aside and enjoy the sweetness and charm of owners Brooke Palance and Michael Wilding, who will win you over the moment you walk in the door. Besides, Brooke's super-nutritious veggie soup is listed as "famous" and you'll want to have it for lunch, often.

The ambience is coffeehouse with lots of eclectic touches that make this place visually interesting. Busts of Italian figures, Baroque angels, and colorful Mexican pottery dot the walls and shelves, and there are two French/Moroccan-like blue lighting fixtures hanging above the order counter adding just the right touch. Not to be outdone by Canyon Road's artsy reputation, the owners have wisely given the walls over to art installations by local artists. Just when you think you've got it all pegged, you spot a paper-doll Elvis shrine on the side of the espresso machine or a Pee-Wee Herman doll hugging one of those Baroque angels, or an Elvis clock with legs and hips swinging to adults-only jazz and rock.

The juxtaposition of "beauty and beast" punk-grunge oddities and elegant stuff works. Where else might you find R. Crumb's candy wrapper design on the "Devil Girl Choco-Bar—It's BAD for you!" with a picture of a naughty, black-haired woman saying "Eat Me" alongside savory stuffed croissants, coconut cream pies, and ginger-lemon cakes.

Of course there's dark, rich espresso drinks, and surprise lunch specials featuring the best, most creative sandwiches in town, plus a great outdoor patio facing Canyon Road that assists uncontrollable people-watchers.

Trixie's has quickly become "the number one place to be" and as their menu says, Trixie's Cafe is "generally a cool place to hang out."

Andiamo!

✪ ✪

322 Garfield. 995-9595.

Chef Christine Galvin

Dinner:	5:30 P.M.-9:30 P.M. Wednesday-Monday. Closed Tuesday.
Features:	Beer/wine. Smoke-free inside. Patio.
Price:	Moderate. Visa/MasterCard.
Cuisine:	Italian. (Menu changes seasonally.)

*A*ndiamo! or "Let's Go" was co-created by former Cafe Escalera sous chef, Chris Galvin, and her business partner, Joan Gillcrist. (Second-generation restaurants have popped up in Santa Fe like sunflowers in a summer field. Many former food-staff members from first-generation restaurants like Santacafé and Cafe Escalara have now opened their own eateries.)

Galvin's experience and knowledge of preparing good, fresh food shows up on the small, daily changing menu. From their previous employers, Galvin and Gillcrist have borrowed a simple philosophy about food and food service that shouts quality.

Emphasis here is Italian— if you haven't already guessed—especially on pastas and beginnings. The *Antipasto* with fresh Mozzarella, hot Coppa (cured Italian ham), roasted peppers, marinated olives, and oven-dried tomatoes is "molto bono" and can be easily shared by two. *Caesar Salad,* or *Crispy Polenta* with Rosemary and Gorgonzola might tempt you instead.

There's a pasta special every night. If the *Cannelloni* are on the menu, get them—two big beautiful, tender pasta tubes stuffed with basil, Mozzarella, and spinach, with a roasted tomato sauce. Divine!

Another great pasta is the *Farfalle* with grilled chicken, spinach, scallions, and Asiago cheese.

The entree I adore and always ask for is the *Chicken Parmesan* with spaghettini, Fontina, and roasted tomato sauce—usually only offered from fall to spring. The *Atlantic Salmon* is ordered a lot by my friends who say it's one of the best in town. A good wine list offers wines that pair with the flavors nicely.

The desserts shine too. The *Polenta Pound Cake* with lemon crema pasticceria (creme anglaise) is exquisite, tender and perfectly right.

Service is capable and unobtrusive. A real plus is the interior refurbishing of the restaurant. Designer Lawrence Standish waved his magic wand and "voila"—rich Tuscan yellows and reds appeared on walls, along with simple but elegant window treatments.

Bon Appetito!

Andiamo!'s Signature Dish

Crispy Polenta with Gorgonzola Sauce

Ingredients for polenta:

3-1/2	*cups salted water*
1	*cup polenta (cornmeal) not instant*
2	*ounces unsalted butter*
	Handful of grated parmesan
1/8	*cup chopped rosemary*
	Red wine, vinegar, salt, and
cayenne	
	Pepper to taste

Method:

Bring water to boil. Slowly whisk in polenta. Cook gently for about 20 minutes. Add the butter, parmesan, rosemary, then red wine, vinegar, salt, and cayenne pepper. Pour polenta into baking pan to 1 to 1-1/2 inches of thickness. Let cool. Slice into desired shape. Cover the bottom of a non-stick sauté pan with olive oil and heat. Fry polenta until crispy. Remove and pat dry.

Ingredients for Gorgonzola sauce:

2	*cups heavy cream*
	Whole sprig of rosemary
	3 to 4 ounces of Gorgonzola
	Salt, black pepper, and lemon juice to taste

Method:

Reduce the heavy cream with rosemary by about one half. Whisk in the Gorgonzola. Season with salt, black pepper, and lemon juice to taste. Pour Gorgonzola sauce into plate and place polenta on top. Garnish with parsley, chives, and bread crumbs.

Yield: 6 to 8 servings.

Atalaya Restaurant & Bakery

320 South Guadalupe. 982-2709.

Breakfast:	7 A.M.-11 A.M. Mon.-Fri.
Lunch:	11 A.M.-5 P.M. Mon.-Fri.
Dinner:	5 P.M.-10 P.M. daily.
Brunch:	7 A.M.-5 P.M. Sat. & Sun.
Features:	Beer/wine. Smoke-free. Smoking permitted on patio. Free parking lot.
Price:	Inexpensive. Major credit cards.
Cuisine:	American.

Atalaya's winning combination: uncomplicated, inexpensive, plus friendly and generous American down-home-good, non-stop service, and just the right amount of Southern and around-the-world cooking to avoid any boredom.

Start breakfast or brunch off with *Blueberry Buttermilk Pancakes* or *Shrimp and Grits,* low country style, with bacon, mushrooms, green onions and hot sauce, served with two fried eggs and toast. What a delightful surprise to see a *Muffuletta* sandwich on the menu! If you've never had one, now's the time to indulge in an old New Orleans tradition—salami, ham, provolone and olive salad wedged between bakery fresh bread and served with a parsley-caper potato salad. The *Caesar Salad with Grilled Chicken Breast* is especially fabulous with it's buttermilk-Maytag Blue Cheese dressing, croutons, and toasted walnuts.

Oriental influences show up in appetizers like *Hong Kong Style Fried Bean Curd* with pickled ginger, scallions, and sesame.

The menu didn't forget some of our favorite New Mexican-slanted dishes like *Atalaya's Cheddarburger* (order green chile on the side) and *Chicken Quesadilla* with Jack cheese, grilled red onion, blackened tomato salsa and sour cream.

Believe it or not you can get all kinds of great coffee drinks, real hot chocolate, sarsparilla floats, best chocolate banana shake, *ever* (to go with that green chile cheeseburger), juices, S. Pellegrino and Tynant waters, root and ginger beers, and soy milk. If that's not enough to titillate your interest, the bakery turns out great crusty loaves (the heavenly *Sourdough Levin and French Baguette* are served to you from large trays throughout your meal) and there's lots of cakes, pastries, and rolls for take-out.

Thank you, John and Murphy O'Brien.

Aztec Cafe

317 Aztec Street. 983-9464.

Breakfast/ Lunch:	7:30 A.M.-9 P.M. Mon.-Thurs. & 7:30 A.M.-11 P.M. Fri.; 8 A.M.-11 P.M. Sat. & 8 A.M.-9 P.M. Sun.
Features:	Beer. Smoking/non-smoking. Patio. Free parking lot. Art. [Historical]
Price:	Budget/Inexpensive. No credit cards.
Cuisine:	American.

A real, hard-core coffeehouse, tucked away on little Aztec Street in a building over 100-years-old, harbors some of the best cappuccinos and lattes in Santa Fe. File past the youthful-dead, black-clad, tattooed twenty-somethings who literally hang over and around the front porch and side patio. And take an empty seat (if you can find one). Not only can you sip your favorite brew before strolling and shopping the Guadalupe area, you can get some tasty *Focaccia Pizza, Egg Salad on Toast, Bagels and Cream Cheese,* and hot soups in the winter. It's also good to know the Aztec uses only Guittard chocolate for their hot chocolates and mochas. Avoid sitting in the smoking room (if you do, you'll know why the young locals call it "The Ashtray") and go for the patio.

Small but serious art shows continue to happen here.

Corn Dance Cafe

1501 Paseo de Peralta (In The Hotel Santa Fe). 982-1200.

Chef Loretta Barrett Oden

Breakfast: 7 A.M.-10 A.M. Mon.-Fri.; 7 A.M.-11 A.M. Sat. & Sun.
Lunch: 11:30 A.M.-2 P.M. Tues.-Sat.
Dinner: 5:30 P.M.-9 P.M. Tues.-Sat.
Native American
Barbeque: 6 P.M.-8 P.M. Friday only.
Features: Full bar. Smoking/non-smoking. Patio.
Price: Moderate. Major credit cards.
Cuisine: Native American.

Creator of the Corn Dance Cafe, Loretta Barrett Oden, is to be applauded for this interesting and successful experiment with Native American cuisine. The cafe is now located within the walls of Santa Fe's only Native American-owned hotel, The Hotel Santa Fe. Native American cuisine is a difficult one to tackle since there are thousands of tribal cuisines across the United States. So, to honor all tribes, Barret Oden uses ingredients that are indigenous to the Americas—North and South. Chiles of course. And pumpkins, squashes, berries, nuts, beans—and last, but not least, corn. Buffalo and wild turkey are also featured.

All this may sound serious, but quite the contrary. The menu offers-up some not-so-serious-sounding dishes like *Kickass Buffalo Chile* in a jalapeño bread bowl and *Little Big Pies,* unusual and exotic pizza-like creations with assortments of meats and/or vegetables placed on top of bread dough and baked. Build-your-own Little Big Pies is offered at breakfast along with a more standard breakfast buffet.

The *Buffalo Burger, Pan-Roasted Medallions of Free Range Turkey* with cranberry-piñon sauce and cornbread dressing, and *Lummi Island Crab Cakes* are jewels in the crown of this cafe. Summer barbeques happen Fridays on the patio when you can expect *Smoked Buffalo Brisket, Achiote Marinated Grilled Chicken,* and lots of grilled vegetables like squash, corn, and potatoes.

Plus: A real horno (an outside adobe oven used by the Pueblo Indians to bake breads) near the patio features Picuris Pueblo bread-baking Saturday mornings 8 A.M.-11 P.M. And there's Native American dances from 5:45 P.M.-6:15 P.M. Saturday evenings.

Cowgirl Hall of Fame

319 South Guadalupe Street. 982-2565.

Lunch:	11 A.M.-4 P.M. daily.
Dinner:	4:30 P.M.-11 P.M. Sun.-Thurs.; 4:30 P.M.- midnight Fri. & Sat.
Features:	Full bar. Smoking/non-smoking. Patio.
Price:	Inexpensive/Moderate. Major credit cards.
Cuisine:	American Barbeque. (Menu changes seasonally.)

*T*here's not much that this New York clone-implant has missed. Their extensive menus for brunch, lunch, and dinner take time to peruse.

Cute headlines indicate what's what: Finger Lickers: *Frito Pie* (a New Mexican odd-ball dish that is oddly-enough, good), *Texas Onion Loaf, Fried Catfish Fingers, Chicken Wang Dangs;* Salad Basket: *Cowgirl Salad* and *Chimayo Chicken Salad;* Sandwiches: *B-B-Q Chicken/Beef on a Bun* and *Catfish Po'Boy;* Chicken Coop: *Honey Fried Chicken, Chicken Fried Chicken, Cowgirl Chicken Fajitas;* Stockyards: *Bunkhouse Smoked Brisket, Smoked Spare Ribs, Chicken Fried Steak, Saddle-up Sirloin Strip*—can we stop now?

The only difference in the lunch and dinner menu is about two to five dollars. The tender, tangy brisket is available by the pound and I recommend stopping by to get some to go—it makes up great sandwiches for lunch or dinner.

The Cowgirl Hall of Fame's night-life scene is very popular. The bar is cozy and rustic, the crowd is friendly—and the music can be great.

Get this: "Deserts" on the menu really means desserts and, can you believe—*Cowgirl's Original Ice Cream Baked Potato?* I think you have the idea, so park your steed and ramble on in for a family fun food fiesta.

Plus: The patio is big, shady, accessible, and very casual.

The Double A

⚫⚫

331 Sandoval Street. 982-8999.

Lunch:	11:30 A.M-2 P.M. Tues.-Fri.
Dinner:	6 P.M.-10 P.M. Tues.-Sun. Closed Monday.
Bar Menu:	6 P.M.-11 P.M. Tues.-Sun. Dinner available in the bar.
Features:	Full bar. Smoke free dining room.
	Smoking permitted in bar. Art. Free parking lot.
Price:	Expensive/Very Expensive. Major credit cards.
Cuisine:	Contemporary American. (Menu changes seasonally.)

Amid all the hubbub of Santa Fe's busy restaurant scene, yet another restaurant opened its doors—or rather grand revolving glass doors with fancy bronze-horn door handles. The Double A quickly created quite a buzz with its bold and daring architecture that had locals instantly loving it or hating it.

Inside, front and center, there's a grand reception desk and to the left a spectacular ash wood bar that sits several steps above the dining area. The bar is complete with ultra-comfortable bar stools (visualize mini-wing-chairs) and is crowned overhead with a chandelier-tangle of bleached antlers. Wizardly bartenders serve up some of the best-in-town hand-shaken margaritas, icy martinis, and divine Cosmopolitan Cocktails (in those elegant long-stemmed glasses) that have ultimately won over a lot of sophisticated elbow-benders.

The gigantic booths (they seat six to eight) that line the sides of the dining room and the *tête-à-tête* seating in roomy, leather wing-chairs near the fireplace are winning combinations. Take a moment to gaze at the glorious painting of a white horse hanging on the bar's north wall by artist Joe Andoe that has become a Double A logo; and the glass-enclosed boxes in every booth displaying artistic and historic memorabilia. Double A has also provided a "chef's table" adjacent to the kitchen that you can reserve for those gourmandise evenings.

This city-fied environment delights the senses, not only with the space but with an up-scale American menu. *The Double A Salad* with bibb lettuce and Maytag blue cheese-buttermilk dressing is simply wonderful. I often get this as my main entree with the soup of the day and a side of their fantastic buttermilk-dipped onion rings. Main entrees change daily or weekly and include some fine dishes like *Venison Andouille Sausage* with red beans and rice and stewed okra; *Seared Swordfish* with quinoa pilaf and roasted vegetable ragout; *Sauteed Veal Scallopine* with cappellini, chives, sugar peas, and white wine; moist, plump, juicy *Chicken—*

just-plucked from a swirling rotisserie—served with mashed potatoes, roasted garlic, and fresh vegetables; and *Grilled Beef Tenderloin* with grilled Portobello mushroom, white truffle potato cake and red wine sauce.

The pastry chef has done a brilliant job creating some of the best desserts in town to end your meal. *Lemon-Ginger Meringue Pie* is extraordinary—perfect in fact—and torched to order. It resembles a flying buttress and is of great proportions. The old-fashioned coconut-white chocolate *Prairie Wedding Cake,* resplendent with icing roses, is perfect for a birthday or special celebration and can be ordered by the slice. Or with a 24-hour notice, you can get the whole cake.

Service can be inconsistent—from friendly and knowledgeable to a bit chilly and uneven. So put on your warm sense of humor before entering. (Definitely not a place for kids.) The over-the-top adult sensibility is actually refreshing after a day with the little ones. You may even reminisce about what it was like to be a grown-up before America threw out the manual on socially correct behavior.

The Double A is also a great place to stop in after hours for a sensational finish to an already great evening. End with a nightcap from their confidently-presented and extensive bar menu: wines, brandies, cognacs, ports, single-malt scotches, ports, sherrys, coffees, dessert wine, rums, and grappas.

What it all boils down to is that Double A is *the* restaurant of the moment and offers a highbrow place to eat, drink, and be worldly.

A Bar (At The Double A)

331 Sandoval Street. 982-8999.

Hours:	8 P.M.-2 A.M. Tues.-Sat.
Features:	Bar menu. Live music with cover. Smoking. Cigar friendly. Free parking lot. Art.
Price:	Moderate/Expensive. Major credit cards.

*T*his latest addition to Double A, connected to the restaurant itself, is a red, romantic lounge that could be a cross between a 1920s Chicago bordello and a New York skyscraper bar. It's plush, it's comfortable, it's outrageous. Exuding high-class, mixed with an air of excitement, the A Bar attracts pleasure-seekers of all ages.

The faux-leopard skin chairs, art-deco chandeliers, walls covered with red-flocked material and just-right "let's get-sexy" paintings, a glossy, black baby-grand piano to accompany the likes of Herbie Mann and Bruce Dunlap "live," and piped-in Ella Fitzgerald, or off-center, kinky organ music, and thick, hazy smoke curling up from chic tables all set the tone for a clubby, in-the-know, mentality. You half expect Bette—Davis *or* Midler—to walk through the very expensive etched-glass doors—oversized of course—exclaiming, "Fasten your seat belts, darling, it's going to be a very bumpy evening."

Cocktails and champagne flow like rivers from the elegant, semi-circular bar backed with more etched-glass. Black tie and long, sweeping gowns wouldn't be out of place here—but since this *is* Santa Fe, just about anything goes.

Pásale Bakery

328 S. Guadalupe Street. 988-5155.

Breakfast/
Lunch: 7 A.M.-6 P.M. daily.
Features: No alcohol. Smoke-free. Patio. Free parking lot.
Price: Budget/Inexpensive. Visa/MasterCard.
Cuisine: American/English/New Mexican.

Yet another tribute to the coffeehouse/cafe scene that is very much alive and well in Santa Fe. This Zia Diner spin-off became popular the minute its doors opened. This year the bakery got a new name and new owners, Jill and Luis Olivas. They have kept a lot of the baked goods that Santa Feans have counted on for many years and added some new ones of their own. Their English and New Mexican roots show up in the form of *Blueberry Lemon Scones* and *Mexican Sweet Breads.* (An English afternoon tea may be forthcoming.)

Located in the hub of the South Guadalupe area, Pasale Bakery sits across the street from the Jean Cocteau Cinema, Santa Fe's beloved artsy movie theatre.

Light lunches, espresso, cappuccinos, breads, cookies, pastries, cakes, and pies are available all day long.

By the way, the Spanish word *Pásale* extends a friendly greeting to customers to "come on in."

Portare Via Italian Cafe

500 Montezuma Street. 988-3886.

Breakfast/ *Lunch:*	7:30 A.M.-6 P.M. Mon-Sat, & 12 P.M.-5 P.M. Sun.
Features:	No alcohol. Smoke-free. Eat in or take out. Free parking lot.
Price:	Inexpensive. Major credit cards.
Cuisine:	Italian.

Sit on the raised seating area overlooking the mall traffic and munch on really good pizzas (same as parent Pranzo's) fired up to order (there are seventeen *extras* that you could add to practically anything on the menu).

Spinaci (the best hot spinach sandwich ever made on their own focaccia), generous, fresh salads like the *Portare Via*—mixed baby greens, roasted chicken, artichoke hearts, bell peppers, red onion, pine nuts, and provolone, and a soup of the day.

If you're up early for the farmer's market (held outside in the Sanbusco parking lot in summer) or shopping, drop in for breakfast. There's a nice assortment of rolls, muffins, scones, croissants, coffee brownies, cinnamon rolls (not those soft, gooey ones, either) breakfast burritos, espressos, cappuccinos, hot chocolates, and yogi lattes.

The sumptuous *Mocha Crema* reminds you of those coffeehouse drinks in San Francisco—just enough coffee, fat, and chocolate to ward off cold, foggy nights. Several other beverages round out the drinks including Italian flavored syrups, juices, sodas, and teas. Plus: All drinks are available with whole or skim milk or in regular or decaffeinated, to stay or to go.

Any pizza on the menu is available in its "pre-baked" form to take home and finish in your own oven. And there's also whole, rosemary-garlic rotisserie chickens to take home, as well.

Pranzo Italian Grill

✪

540 Montezuma Street. 984-2645.

Chef Cy Yontz

Lunch:	11:30 A.M.-3 P.M. Mon.-Sat.
Dinner:	5 P.M.-10 P.M. Sun.-Thurs.; 5 P.M.-11 P.M. Fri. & Sat.
Bar menu:	12 P.M.-midnight Mon.-Sat.; 12 P.M.-10 P.M. Sunday.
Rooftop menu:	11:30 A.M.-3 P.M. & 5 P.M.-10 P.M Sun.-Thurs.; 5 P.M.-11 P.M. FRI. & SAT.
Features:	Full bar. Smoking/nonsmoking. Patio & rooftop terrace. Free parking lot.
Price:	Moderate/Expensive. Major credit cards.
Cuisine:	Italian.

Pranzo offers a stylish bar, rooftop dining, thin-crust pizzas, big salads, sandwiches, over eight pastas, grilled fish, chicken, beef, and daily specials—all for reasonable prices. Comfortable, gray booths line the walls, and white linens and butcher paper-covered tables are spaced nicely around the dining room.

Don't rule out the bar/lounge for dining—it's classy. The bathrooms are a kick—Italian language lessons are piped in just in case you've recently booked a trip to Florence.

Pranzo's offers a lot of classic Italian dishes that are good old standbys—ones I never tire of. For example, appetizers I love to order are the *Fritto Misto con Salsa Picante,* fried shrimp, calamari, and scallops flanked by a ramekin of spicy tomato sauce to dip them in; and *Carpaccio* (paper-thin sliced raw beef drizzled with an excellent olive oil—Pranzo's white truffle oil—with shaved aged "grana" cheese from Italy and cracked black pepper over all.)

A salad favorite, especially when "doing lunch with the girls" is the *Pranzo Insalata* (all the menu headings are in Italian) a good-size plate of baby greens, radichio, hearts of palm, Roma tomatoes, Gorgonzola, salami, and Balsamic vinaigrette. The pasta *Linguini con Salsiccia* featuring Pranzo's house-made sausage, roasted bell peppers, basil, and tomato sauce is always good. The *Ravioli di Ricotta e Spinaci alla Crema di Salvia* (spinach and Ricotta ravioli with sage cream sauce) can be very good but since it's on the rich side, the *Insalata di Acciuga* or Caesar style salad is in order.

Other favorties at lunch are two sandwiches—the *Panini Bistecca*—juicy, sliced grilled sirloin with rosemary, olive oil, and black pepper on Pranzo's own foccacia. If they're doing them right, the foccacia should be grilled as well. The other one is the *Mezza Pollo*, a grilled chicken breast with smoked bacon, Roma tomatoes, Fontina, and basil aioli, all layered between the foccacia. One of my lunch partners always orders the *Mezza Pollo* with the foccacia on the side; it arrives looking more like a dinner entree and is just as appealing. Thin, crispy, house-made potato chips and pasta salad come with the sandwiches making this a hearty lunch. The quality of sandwiches has been inconsistent in the past, but the last *Panini Bistecca* I had was perfect.

Starting off dinner with a pizza as an appetizer is a fine idea and gives everyone a chance to sample some of the best thin-crust pizzas in town. The *Pizza con Salsiccia* with roasted garlic puree, Pranzo's house-made sausage, mushrooms and two cheeses, Gorgonzola and Mozzarella, is an excellent choice, not to mention the very classic *Pizza Margherita* with tomato sauce, Mozzarella, and basil. Magnifico! (I find if I order a thin-crust pizza with too many ingredients on top, it can become soggy.)

Pastas at dinner are the same as lunch, but are about two dollars more per entree. The *Griglia* part of the menu expands to seven entrees and includes a *Delizie del Mercato,* assorted grilled seasonal vegetables—something Italian cooking always does well. The *Pollastrino Arrosto,* oven roasted chicken in natural *jus* is a nice balance between crispness and softness and comes with a decent Parmesan Orzo and grilled vegetables. *Osso Bucco Milanese* is on the winter menu; and the *Tacchino Piccata,* pan-seared turkey, with a light, lemony sauce of lemon, capers, and parsley, served with roasted garlic mashed potatoes is always available. Fish and seafood show up every day on the menus and the *Char-grilled Tuna* with a brandy, peppercorn cream sauce may be available.

The wine selections are thoughtful with many fine Italian wine choices. Four dessert standards are always available: a *Creme Brulee* (the flavor changes daily), *Tiramisu* (holding first place in popularity), *Gelatie Sorbetto,* assorted ice creams and sorbets with biscotti, and *Amaretti con Vin Santo,* a biscotti, perfect for dipping into the glass of dessert wine.

Pranzo is sooooo Italian.

Tomasita's

---

500 S. Guadalupe Street. 983-5721.

Lunch/Dinner: **11 A.M.-10 P.M. Mon.-Sat. Closed Sunday.**
Features: **Full bar. Smoking/nonsmoking. Patio.**
                    Free parking lot. [Historical]
Price: **Inexpensive. Visa/MasterCard.**
Cuisine: **New Mexican.**

*H*oused in an old railyard warehouse, Tomasita's is *the* most popular New Mexican eatery around, even though it may not be the best. Tomasita's popularity demands a huge waiting area where you might wait over an hour, especially in the peak season months.

They crank out fiery chile and daily specials here with remarkable and phenomenal speed to keep up with the crowds. After orders are placed, food is presented within ten minutes. If you can tolerate smoke, sit in the bar that vacates more quickly. My favorite dish is their bowl of green with beans, cheese, and sour cream (you'll need the sour cream to cut the heat). Its hot and hearty and comes with a sopaipilla. (Tomasita's banner sopaipillas are right up there with the best.)

Honey is on every table in squeeze-containers for their hot, puffy, deep-fried versions of flatbread. Did you know that honey, sugar, or salt tames chile's heat? If you get severely burned, immediately coat your tongue with one of the above. Forget gulping your frosty margarita—it really doesn't work as well, even if it is more fun.

Daily specials are a good bargain and the combination plates give you a taste of almost everything. Vegetarians will make out just fine.

It is strongly recommended that you try to eat here at an off-hour, say around 3 or 4 P.M. to avoid the extra-heavy crush of traffic in the summer.

Zia Diner

326 S. Guadalupe Street 988-7008.

Lunch/Dinner: 11:30 A.M.-10 P.M. daily.
Features: Full bar. Smoking/non-smoking. Patio.
             Free parking lot.
Price: Inexpensive/Moderate. Major credit cards.
Cuisine: American.

The Zia Diner, in the tradition of all good diners, delivers the goods. The Zia's *Meatloaf,* embedded with green chile, pine nuts, and herbs with lumpy, real mashed potates and gravy, vegetables, and warm bakery rolls with butter, shines as their most popular diner dish. And it's an incredible bargain at lunch or dinner— just $6.25.

The *Chicken Fried Steak* and their *Chicken Fried Chicken* has just the right amount of deep-fried crunch and come with the same scrumptious mashed potatoes, gravy, rolls, and vegetables. Try the winning *Cobb Salad* heaped with bacon, avocado, turkey, blue cheese, and eggs—and, of course, some greens underneath. Cheeseburger? It passes the diner check list with flying colors. Get the chile-cheese-burger.

Daily specials include fresh fish, pastas, and soups. And there are Blue Plate specials Monday through Sunday. Dinner specials stray from the pure diner path and tend to be too upscale-fussy. But the real diner dishes are still here.

Fruit pies (strawberry-rhubarb), chocolate cakes, malts, and milkshakes complete the picture. The *hot fudge sundae* features housemade fudge sauce that is dark, bitterweet, shiny and luscious—and the whole thing is slathered with whipped cream, capped with a bright red cherry!

Plus: You can sit on an old-fashioned barstool at the curvy 50s bar and watch the kitchen staff scramble while you down good ol' diner grub.

Bagelmania

420 Catron Street. 982-8900.
Second location next to Pier 1 Imports, Cerrillos and Rodeo Roads.

Breakfast/Lunch: 7 A.M.-2 P.M. Mon.-Fri.; 7 A.M.-3 P.M. Sat. & Sun.
Bakery/Deli hours: 7 A.M.-6 P.M. Mon.-Sat.; 7 A.M.-3 P.M. Sun.
Features: Smoke-free. No alcohol. Smoking permitted on patio. Free parking lot.
Price: Budget/Inexpensive. Visa/MasterCard.
Cuisine: Jewish delicatessen.

*T*hird generation bagel-makers from New York, the Schwartzberg family, landed in Santa Fe bringing along slogans such as "If a seagull flies over the sea, what flies over the bay?" and "Anything you can finagel, I'll put on a bagel."

Using the Broadway-style deli motif, Bagelmania turns out mighty good bagels and *Chicken Soup with Matza Balls* in this industrial, bright, clattery, usually-packed, place. There's lots of overstuffed sandwiches to choose from as well as Platters in the Round that feature *Smoked Fish Platter* with bagel or bialy, cream cheese or butter served with lettuce, tomato, olive, onion, and cucumber; or *Nova Scotia Platter,* or *Whitefish Platter,* or *Baked Salmon Platter*—all deluxe, the menu says.

If that's not enough smoked fish, try the *Jacques Cousteau*—a platter for smoked-fish lovers. *Marilyn Monroe* and *John Wayne* show up as meat and cheese plates, and *Tom Mix* as a chef's salad.

The menu is big and broad like the humor, and tempts with all kinds of salads: egg, chicken, chopped liver, and tuna—with a supporting cast of slaw, pickles, applesauce, Nova, cream cheese, and knishes.

Don't forget to order an egg cream or Dr. Brown's Celery Soda. The take-out counters are busy, but stop at the bakery counter for an order of *rugglah* to go with next morning's coffee.

So, new? What flies over the bay? A *bagel,* you ninny.

Bert's Burger Bowl

235 N. Guadalupe Street. 982-0215.

Lunch/Dinner:	**10:30 A.M.-7:45 P.M. Mon.-Sat.;**
	10:30 A.M.-5:45 P.M. Sun.
Features:	**No alcohol. Patio. Free parking lot.**
Price:	**Budget. Visa/MasterCard.**
Cuisine:	**American.**

Certainly a Santa Fe tradition—maybe because it's been here so long. The few stone tables outside replaced the old aluminum ones and have been updated with canvas market umbrellas. As far as modernizing, that's where the buck stops.

The tiny inside is mostly kitchen where the old fashioned char-broiled burgers—seven kinds in all—have been served to faithful locals for over forty years. The burgers are quarter-pound, the cheese is American, the buns are white. So it's a good idea to wash it all down with a French coke (vanilla syrup is added).

If you must stray from the tried and true, there's fried chicken by the piece or a full dinner. You can have ham, tuna, and egg sandwiches, bean, avocado, or carnitas burritos, menudo, posole, tacos, chicken flautas, fries, and onion rings.

Best here is the chile-cheeseburger with French coke. Easy on the pocketbook and kid-friendly.

Il Vicino

321 W. San Francisco Street. 986-8700.

Managing Partner: Eric Segura

Lunch/Dinner:	11:30 A.M.-11 P.M. Sun.-Thurs.; 11:30 A.M.-midnight Fri.-Sat.
Features:	Beer/wine. Smoke-free. Smoking permitted on patio. Free parking lot.
Price:	Inexpensive. Major credit cards.
Cuisine:	Italian.

*P*IZZA served piping from a red-hot, wood-fired oven that is located near the back door is the main feature here—with ten pizzas to choose from.

There's a bar in front of the oven that sits in the back of a long, narrow room so you can watch the pizza guys make yours to order. And if it's a cold day, the comfort of the fire is a plus. An in-house brewery serves up *Il Vicino Ale* by glass or gallon if wine doesn't suit you.

Ordering is walk-up-to-the-counter simple and the goods are delivered to your table. All pizzas are 10-inches and the place is open late—a rarity in Santa Fe.

Salads are big enough for lunch or dinner and can be split with a friend. Favorites here are the *Insalata Il Vicino,* with chicken, Gorgonzola, artichoke hearts, eggs, tomatoes, walnuts, and romaine salad; and the *Pesto Pizza* with fresh basil pesto, sundried tomatoes, Mozzarella, pine nuts, and fresh tomatoes.

The ever-classic *Pizza Margherita* is adorned with tomato sauce, Mozzarella, and fresh basil. Ordering this is a good way to test the quality of their kitchen. If they can make this one well, you know you're on the right track.

The atmosphere is stylish, contemporary Italian. With fun, modern fixtures, plates and platters in colorful Fiestaware, and deep reds and light ochres on walls, as well as in Italian cherub pictures—Il Vicino stands apart from your ordinary "pizza parlor."

La Bell's

---

301 Jefferson Street (at N. Guadalupe). 986-8223.

Breakfast/
Lunch: 7 A.M.-5 P.M. Mon-Fri & 10 A.M.-4 P.M. Sat. Closed Sun.
Features: No alcohol. Drive-up. Inside/Outside seating.
Price: Budget. No credit cards.
Cuisine: New Mexican.

*F*ormer owners of Maria Ysabel's have kept some of their old favorite recipes alive and added more: *Breakfast Burritos* with eggs, potatoes, cheese, bacon, sausage, or chorizo fills your empty energy tank. Or how about a *Breakfast Burger* with sausage patty, egg, red or green chile, and cheese on a grilled hamburger bun? (Beats the Big M.)

A favorite lunch: the *Carne Adovada Burrito*. It's prepared with beans and cheese but you can special-order it—with or without the beans and/or cheese. I like it with just the tender meat that is like an old-fashioned brisket, but here it's slow-cooked in a chile sauce. You may want to ask for it by the pound for those late-night sandwiches.

There's also an unusual *Meatball Burrito* with red or green chile and cheese that's really worth a try. Quesadillas, tacos, tostadas, and a *Foot-Long Hot Dog* with cheese and Bell's special chile sauce, are also offered. If you stick with the *Carne Adovada Burrito,* you won't be sorry.

Noon Whistle

---

451 W. Alameda Street. 988-2636.

Lunch: 10 A.M.-3 P.M. Mon.-Fri.
Features: No alcohol. Patio. Smoke-free. Free parking lot.
Price: Budget/Inexpensive. No credit cards.
Cuisine: American.

*T*he big thing here is the sandwiches—for here or to go. Be prepared to wait—the menu asks that you allow 15-20 minutes because they're all made fresh to order. (I found the wait to be more like 10 minutes.) The Noon Whistle has always been packed with working folks who have enjoyed lunch here for many years.

Those in the know enter in through the back door where the narrow, wood platform-patio and parking lot are located. Order at the counter from menus that are posted on a bulletin board and the counter itself. Pay the cashier, and wait for your name to be called out.

The atmosphere is friendly—amid grand funk from the exposed electrical lines down to the spotted, dark gray carpet that lines the simple dining room. The Noon Whistle consists of one big room that's heated by an old wood stove and divided into two sections: a cashier/soup/coffee counter and some slap-dash shelving that holds small bags of potato chips, and this 'n that. Behind the shelving is a hard-working sandwich maker who might remind you of an auntie you once knew who could make a terrific sandwich—you know, unadorned and just like the kind of lunch sandwiches you remember from childhood.

Perfectly crisp bacon is piled up on the grill ready for the next *BLT* or *New Club,* a one-layered affair with turkey, bacon, melted Jack, mayo, lettuce, and tomato on a hot French roll (mustard and onion must be requested). Most of the sandwiches come whole or half and offer choices of breads: whole wheat, French roll, seven-grain, and rye. There's always a soup of the day along with several salads, drinks, and three desserts: cookie, brownie, or pie.

Tired of those complex Southwestern flavors and high lunch tabs? Give your pocketbook and tummy a rest—get the *Cold Turkey Sandwich* piled high with fresh sprouts on seven-grain or a *Cheeseburger* with pickle on a whole wheat bun for $3.25. Yes, I said $3.25.

Pizza, Etc.

★

151 Paseo de Peralta, De Vargas Center. 986-1500.

Lunch/Dinner:	11 A.M.-8 P.M. Mon.-Sat.; 11 A.M.-9:30 P.M. Fri.; 12 P.M.-8 P.M. Sun.
Features:	Beer/wine. Nonsmoking. Free parking lot.
Price:	Inexpensive. No credit cards.
Cuisine:	Italian/American.

Don't turn your nose up at this mall restaurant or you'll be missing a good thing. Chef-owners Roland Richter and his wife, Sheila Nixon, have opened up a gourmet pizza fast-food-in-the-mall restaurant —with take-out/counter service— that features made-to-order gourmet pizzas and house-made desserts. Pizza, Etc. was recently named one of the top-hundred independent pizza restaurants across America by the trade publication, *Pizza Today.*

The restaurant is mostly an open kitchen with a counter and seven tables lined up against the wall facing the movie theatres. A canopy covers most of the tables and there's a railing so you feel safely separated from the movie mobs. Shakers of Parmesan and crushed chile pepper are on every table. It's too bad that the serviceware is strickly paper and plastic—pizzas tend to get soggy quickly, and cappuccino stays blistering hot in those paper cups.

Pop in before or after the movies, or just pop in, and try one of Richter's house special pizzas like the *Pizza Giovanni* with Montrachet goat cheese, roasted sweet red peppers, fresh roasted garlic, and fresh oregano; or the *Pontchartrain* topped with Andouille sausage, shrimp, caramelized onions, and scallions; or the *Oysters Rockefeller Pizza* with oysters, sambuca, and spinach on bechamel sauce.

Can you believe? *The New Mexican Pizza* with refried beans, salsa, green chile, corn, Mozzarella and Cheddar cheeses. Sandwiches and subs on house-baked focaccia, two pastas, and five salads are here as well. If your taste runs to more classic pizzas like cheese and pepperoni (lavishly covered with large slices of pepperoni) they're all here. Crusts are thin and toppings generous. A diagram on the wall shows you the size of a slice or whole pizza—the slice *is* big.

Being a sucker for *banana cream pie* and seeing it on the chalkboard, I had to try it. It's house-made and delivers fresh bananas in a creamy vanilla filling cloaked with real whipped cream Or try their *Zabaglione* with pizzelle (waffle-like crisp cookie) and fresh berries; or the *Wild Rice Pudding.*

Poulet Patate Rotisserie

⊗

446 West San Francisco Street. 820-2929.

Chef: Zabie Vourvoulis

Brunch:	10:30 A.M.-3 P.M. Sat. & Sun.
Lunch:	11:30 A.M.-2:30 P.M. Mon-Fri.
Dinner:	6 P.M.-9:30 P.M. Sun.-Thurs.; 6 P.M.-10 P.M. Fri. & Sat.
Takeout:	Lunch & Dinner hours—call ahead to order. Catering available.
Features:	Special Holiday Menus. Beer/wine. Smoke-free. Patio. Free parking lot.
Price:	Moderate/Expensive. Major credit cards.
Cuisine:	French Rotisserie.

*T*he South of France has come to Santa Fe via third-generation French restaurateur, co-owner Zabie, *Patronne aux Fourneaux,* and executive chef of Poulet Patate—a place that specializes in spit or fire-roasted, herbes de Provence-coated rotisserie chickens. The original, funky building has been gutted and transformed into a charming, full-of-light, French country-style eatery boasting a huge six-by-six-foot wood burning rotisserie that holds seventy-two birds at once and is centered in a big rustic, open kitchen.

As soon as you walk through the handsome doors sporting ironwork in the shape of a chicken, you might sense something good is about to happen. Inside and above the opening to the dining areas are these words, stenciled in arched rows overhead: *"Vivez Heureux Aujourd'Hui, Car Demain Il Sera, Trop Tard."* Translation: "Live happily today because tomorrow it will be too late." I can assure you that you will live a little happier if you partake of Zabie's authentic, fresh and simple, but well done, fare.

To insure that the ingredients used in her cooking are organic and ultra fresh, it is Poulet Patate's policy to puchase natural meats and organic or unsprayed produce from local sources whenever possible.

The interior is warm sienna-to-viridian hand-stained walls, with comfortable chairs, and bistro-style tables covered with Souleiado Provençal oilcloths that appear to bring the sunshine in. There is also an open, glassed terrace for outside dining. Fresh flowers are on every table as well as a big peppermill that you can really use, a large La Baleine sea salt container, and proper, authentic flatware which

Zabie picked out in France "that has shape and balance that applies substance and allows for generous bites."

A lovely dinner for two could start with *Les Croustades*—grilled, crusty bread slices spread with three du jour selections such as tapanade, ratatouille, or a paté and served with a generous portion of braised endive and greens—almost a meal for two, and a generous appetizer for three or four; or a *Mesclun Salad*—mixed baby greens with toasted walnuts and basalmic vinegar; and then go on to perhaps a classic *Onion Soup Gratinee* or *Soupe de Poisson Provençale*—pureed fish soup with garlic, saffron and Pernod served with grilled toasts and rouille. Add one of

those rotisseried entrees, two glasses of *1993 Chateau Fonscolombe, Aix-en-Provence, France,* a caramelized, flaky *Tarte Tatin* and two espressos—voila!—a perfect meal.

The house rotisserie specialty, *Herbs de Provence Chicken,* is a half chicken rubbed and encrusted with the herbs of Provence. Zabie's skill at fire-roasted, rotisseried meats and birds show up on the menu with a Moroccan spice-rubbed *Leg of Lamb* and the *Rotisserie Duck* stuffed with oranges and rosemary and glazed with honey, lavender (the essential herb of Provence), balsamic vinegar, and shallots.

If you prefer something from the grill, the feature here is the *New York Strip Pepper Steak.*

All entrees come with two vegetable accompaniments—the Rouquefort potatoes in the winter, ratatouille in the summer, and braised endive which are, what can I say, "tres divine."

There are great all-vegetable selections such as *Plat Jardinier*—the chef's selection of seasonal, Elizabeth Berry vegetables—or, at lunch, a *Fire-roasted Eggplant and Pepper Sandwich* with goat cheese and sun-dried tomato-basil aioli served with frites or mixed green salad.

◆ North Guadalupe Street Area

Lunch at Poulet Patate is just as good as dinner. The *Poulet Minute*—half a rotisseried chicken with roast potatoes or green salad; or their *Chicken Mango Salad* with rotisserie chicken, mangoes, impeccably fresh baby greens, housemade mayonnaise and walnut oil dressing are high on the list.

Get *Berries on a Cloud* if it's offered on the dessert menu the day you have lunch or dinner. Ooh, la, la!

There is a take-out menu offering the Poulet Minute, the whole rotisserie chicken, or lamb meal with two side dishes. Run home *tout de suite*, light the candles, set out the white linen, open that special bottle of wine you've been harboring—and *bon appetit!*

Vanessie of Santa Fe

434 W. San Francisco Street. 982-9966.

Dinner:	5:30 P.M.-10 P.M. Sun.-Thurs.; 5:30 P.M.-10:30 P.M. Fri. & Sat.
Bar:	4:30 P.M.-1:30 A.M.
Features:	Full bar. Piano bar and bar menu. Smoking/ nonsmoking. Free parking lot. Art. [Historical]
Price:	Moderate/Expensive. Major credit cards.
Cuisine:	American.

The big draw here is the piano bar (said to be one of the ten best piano bars in the world) that swings nightly to nimble hands of pianists, Doug Montgomery and Charles Tichenor. Dated, but fun, the piano bar atmosphere is all ham and corn, naughty but nice.

The locals begin to flock in after 9 P.M., to enjoy music from Brubeck to Bach, Gershwin tunes (Doug sings, too), Broadway musical faves—and to gossip about current events. (If you heard it at Vanessie's in the P.M. you can be sure it will be all over town the next A.M.)

Flanking the end walls of the large-scale bar area are colossal twin fireplaces—architecture by Ron Robles—known for his bigger-than-life spaces. Excessive steel cow skulls hang above each one staring out at the characters that flock here to gab and drink. The black, grand piano takes center attention with numerous tables and director chairs covered in blue canvas placed in comfortable groups for easy listening. The ceilings are about fifteen-feet-high, and the huge mirror behind the piano is at least five-by-six feet.

It's all a bit Bunyanesque, but it works. A bar menu is in place to ensure nibbling and late-night snacks. *Chef's Green Chile Beef Stew*, *Vanessie Burger*, and *Potato Fingers* with ranch peppercorn dipping sauce are some of the ordered-a-lot menu items. "Big" continues to identify the main restaurant with its spectacular high-beamed ceilings and four sets of twelve-foot-high double doors that have five-foot-high glass arched insets in each door. There are some Native American-style paintings and other art adorning walls and shelves. The geometric massiveness of the room is offset by round dining tables—some large enough to accommodate ten place-settings—and chairs, all in blond wood, to lighten things up.

If your appetite is also big, you're in luck, because the portions are huge. Vanessie's dinner menu is simple, classic steakhouse—all a la carte. Out of three starters, the *House Salad* with sizeable slices of white onions and tomatoes sitting on a bed of red-leaf lettuce with sundried tomato vinaigrette topped with Feta cheese, is the best. It's refreshing and is the proper companion to meat. The 16-ounce *New York Sirloin* came a perfect medium and outdid the *Vanessie Ribeye* in flavor and texture The beef is all certified Angus Beef. *Grilled Chicken Breast*, *Rotisserie Chicken*, *Grilled Shrimp*, *New Zealand Rack of Lamb*, *Rock Lobster Tail*, *Surf & Turf*, and a fresh, grilled fish complete the entrees. On the night I dined, the fish was a *farm-raised Salmon Filet*. It was okay, but I'll stick with the steaks, thank you.

Enormous baked potatoes with puzzling, too-salty butter and sour cream on the side can be divided up if you want to share. A scrumptious, mountain-sized *deep-fried onion loaf* will draw happy exclamations! Other sides include sauteed mushrooms and a vegetable of the day.

Pass on the desserts that are made elsewhere unless you just have to have the cheesecake.

That's it. "Big V of Santa Fe."

Whistling Moon Cafe

★ ★

402 N. Guadalupe Street. 983-3093.

Chef Tracy Ritter.

Lunch/Dinner: 11 A.M.-10 P.M. daily.
Features: Beer/Wine. Smoke-free.
Price: Inexpensive. No credit cards.
Cuisine: Mediterranean. (Menu changes seasonally.)

*T*racy Ritter (former executive chef at Santacafé) opened this cafe—one that was a long time coming. And it's now one of my favorite restaurants. A cheery greeting from Ritter and the smell of Mediterranean food wafting from the kitchen make you feel all warm and cozy when you enter this honest, down-to-earth, table-to-table cafe—bustling with lots of locals.

What the heck is Mediterranean cuisine anyway? Well, the food is defined by the sea—the Mediterranean, of course—and the countries that border it. Beginning counterclockwise—Spain, Morocco, Algeria, Tunisia, Libya, Egypt, Israel, Lebanon, Syria, Cyprus, Turkey, Crete, Greece, Albania, Yugoslavia, Italy, Sicily, Sardinia, Corsica, Monaco, France, and the Balearic Islands of Ibiza, Mallorca, and Menorca. Now, when you see the menu at Whistling Moon, you won't be stumped by the seemingly unusual mix of countries and dishes. Fourteen tapas and mezze give a lot of choices for starters, from the simple but properly prepared *hummus to muergez* (spicy Moroccan lamb sausage) to *Fried Calamari with Harissa Aioli.*

The *Vegetarian Grapeleaves* are morsel-marvels filled with pine nuts, currants, pomegranate molasses, and exotic spices (see recipe on page 112). Salad plates are heaped with green—almost to the point of overkill—and piled with things like grilled, fresh tuna for the *Nicoise Salad* (already talked about as the best-in-town), roasted peppers, olives, and Feta cheese on the *Greek Salad,* and another with grilled rosemary chicken, sun-dried tomatoes, shaved fennel, artichokes and Asiago cheese.

The "Sandwiches"—*Pitas* filled with *grilled lamb-burgers, Falafels,* or *Lemon Marinated Chicken;* or the *Pannis* stuffed with grilled fish; or *Rosemary Chicken* with carmelized onions; or *Prosciutto;* or *Caprese* with fresh Mozzarella, tomato

and basil—are flavor wonders. What? More? You bet!

Pizzas or calzones and pastas round out the menu. After 5 P.M. be sure to ask about daily specials: If you're lucky the *Roasted Lamb with Prunes and Olives* will be available (believe me, it gets sold out fast). Grilled fish specials also show up at dinner. Definitely get a side order of their irresistible *Spicy Coriander-Cumin Fries* served with a complex spicy dip or you'll be sorry when you see your neighbors at the next table engaged in a fries-eating-frenzy!

There's one dessert here that must be ordered—even if you must share it with a friend. The *Chocolate Souffle Cake*. It's at once rich and light, melts on your tongue, and is an extremely bittersweet chocolate confection that is served surrounded by a creme anglaise. It can't get any better.

Whistling Moon Cafe's Signature Dish

Vegetarian Grapeleaves

Ingredients for filling:

3/4	white onion, finely chopped
1-1/2	cloves garlic, minced
2	tablespoons olive oil
2-1/2	cups white or brown Basmati rice
1/2	cup pine nuts, lightly toasted
1/2	cup currants or golden raisins
1/4	cup fresh chopped dill
3	tablespoons fresh chopped parsley
2	tablespoons allspice
2	tablespoons cumin
3/4	teaspoon black pepper
1-1/2	teaspoons salt
2	ounces canned or fresh diced tomatoes
1-1/2	teaspoons pomegranate molasses

Ingredients for preparation:

16	ounce jar of grapeleaves
1	cup ketchup
2	cloves garlic, whole

Method *for filling:*

Sauté onion and garlic in oil until very lightly colored. Add rice and cook to coat. Remove from heat, cool slightly, and add remaining ingredients, except grapeleaves, ketchup, and whole garlic cloves.

Remove grapeleaves from jar, rinse under cool water. Snip stems from leaves. Fill with a tablespoon of filling and roll up like a burrito.

Finish:

Place grapeleaves in a pot, cover with water, add ketchup, and 2 additional garlic cloves. Place a plate on top of pot, allowing for some movement as the leaves cook. Bring to boil, reduce to a simmer and cook for about 1 and 1/4 hours. Leaves are done when filling is soft and leaf is somewhat tender.

Remove from heat, remove leaves from pot. Allow to cool slightly and place in a non-reactive bowl or jar. Cover with 3/4 olive oil and 1/4 lemon juice. Grapeleaves will keep for a few days uncooked or cooked covered with the oil and lemon juice.

Yield: 40 grapeleaves

Dave's Not Here

✪

1115 Hickox Street. 983-7060.

Lunch/Dinner: 11 A.M.-10 P.M. Mon.-Sat. Closed Sunday.
Features: Beer/Wine. Smoke-free. Free parking lot.
Price: Budget/Inexpensive. No credit cards.
Cuisine: American/New Mexcian.

*W*hen you phone this restaurant and ask for Dave, guess what the answer is? Doesn't matter because with or without Dave being "here," large portions, and low prices—plus thick, perfectly cooked chile-cheeseburgers and just-the-right-amount-of-fat French fries, and house-made chile rellenos have kept the locals dropping by for over ten years.

Dave's burgers rate high in my book and are among the top-ten best burgers in Santa Fe. And you can't beat the down-to-earth local atmosphere.

La Choza

✪

905 Alarid Street. 982-0909.

Lunch/Dinner: 11 A.M.- 9 P.M. daily. (Check for winter hours.)
Features: Beer/wine. Smoke-free. Smoking permitted on patio.
Free parking lot. [Historical]
Price: Budget/Inexpensive. Major credit cards.
Cuisine: New Mexican.

*A*nother historical building dating back to the turn of the century—this one used to be the bunkhouse and headquarters of the Mercer Ranch. La Choza (loosely translated, "the shed") has got to be one of the best New Mexican restaurants in town. (Their sister restaurant downtown is named, The Shed.)

They don't tell you, but the tortilla chips are made here, thick and crunchy, and come with a good, thick tomatoey house-made salsa. In fact, almost everything is made here. Early in the morning, the chile sauces are prepared fresh, daily. And it shows.

The perfect combination of smooth, sweet, and just-right hotness red chile, and the hot-sweet, tart green must be tasted. Highly recommended is the *#1 Enchilada Plate,* vegetarian or with bits of pork. Ask for both the red and green with your order which is referred to in New Mexico as "Christmas." My friend David Krause always orders the *#3 Taco Plate*—he insists it's the best entree on the menu.

You can't get more New Mexico-traditional when it comes to La Choza's menu: *Blue Corn Tortillas* make up the stacked-or-flat enchiladas served with pinto beans, posole, and iceberg lettuce with bits of tomato. There's soft tacos, tamales, burritos, the ever-present green chile stew with pork and potatoes, and a bowl of green with beans and meat (vegetarian menu can be made on request for this and most entrees).

Skipping dessert would be an error considering they do make their own: Try the rich *Coffe/Chocolate Mocha Cake* topped with real, not-from-a-can, whipped cream or the *Hot Fudge Sundae*—they make their own dark chocolate fudge. The *Red Raspberry Sundae's* no slouch either.

Daily specials appear on a small blackboard in the cashier's area, and there's a sign asking you to wait to be seated.

Two big dining rooms are typical old Santa Fe-style with heavy vigas, brick floors, graceful connecting archways, and gay primary colors that warm up stark white walls. Faux-painted shutters and stylized flowers surround windows and flow over arches. Spanish tunes add the proper musical background.

A not-to-be-missed mural: "The Three Graces" dance their way across the ladies' room wall. Check out the vivid lime-green paint job.

Tourists often pass this place by, and that's too bad. It's better than most—and the prices will make you shout for joy.

Masa Sushi

Solana Shopping Center. 927 W. Alameda. 982-3334.

Lunch:	11 A.M.-2 P.M. Mon.-Fri.
Dinner:	5:30 P.M.-9:30 P.M. daily.
Features:	Beer/wine. Smoke-free. Free parking lot.
Price:	Moderate/Expensive. Visa/MasterCard.
Cuisine:	Japanese.

Do you love sushi, still, after all these years? Good news if you do. Master Sushi Chef, Masa-san (who used to preside over and prepare sushi for Shoko-Cafe and then operated a tiny sushi bar in The Country Store on Old Las Vegas Highway) has opened his own sushi bar and restaurant in the Solana Shopping Center.

Thankfully, the interior has been redone and a sushi bar added, complete with a wood-trellised veranda overhead. It's clean, it's charming, and it's darn good.

There are over fifty a la carte sushi items (two pieces per order) and Masa-san will prepare any sushi to order.

There are crunchy sushis: *Spider*—filled with soft-shelled crab; a toothsome *Yellow Tail (deep fried)* —the fish is surrounded with crunchy white rice; *Santa Fe Roll* includes several, tiny, crispy brown shrimp that peek out from the top of the roll. And then there's the *Sweet Shrimp (ama ebi)*—costs you extra for the fried heads; *Smelt Egg (masaqo)*, *Octopus (tako)*, *Sea Eel (anaqo)*, and the mandatory *Sea Urchin (uni)*.

Besides all this sushi, some of the fifteen appetizers are quite good: *Spicy Tuna Salad* (tuna with spice) is a winner—lots of raw tuna with spicy dressing and daikon radish. Six Korean dishes complement the menu. (Masa-san and his wife, who runs the kitchen, are originally from Korea.) There are sashimi and sushi bar entrees as well. There's also two Chinese dishes, six additional Japanese entrees and three nabe dishes—*Sukiyaki, Nabeyaki-Udon,* and *Tempura-Udon.* Note: Appetizer number 7—*Karamari*—is calamari.

The only downside here is the service. It can be very slow. So be prepared— and be patient.

Tiny's Restaurant & Lounge

1015 Pen Road Shopping Center
(St. Francis at Cerrillos Intersection). 983-9817.

Lunch:	11:30 A.M.-2 P.M. Mon.-Sat. Closed Sunday.
Features:	Full bar. Smoking/nonsmoking. Patio. Free parking lot.
Price:	Inexpensive/Moderate. Major credit cards.
Cuisine:	New Mexican.

*O*ver forty years in the restaurant business says something: Tiny's is certainly one of the "old boy" places serving up straight-forward New Mexican favorites without gimmicks or frills. *Money* magazine once called Tiny's "a best kept secret."

Like a lot of the older Santa Fe eateries, it has a dark bar and lounge that you can drink and eat in; and another, brighter dining area for those who prefer that atmosphere.

Waitresses are friendly and have been serving some of the same folks for a very long time. Tiny's is off the tourist map, but if you want a real hit of New Mexico, this is it—with classic New Mexican dishes heading the menu.

Tiny's will accommodate large parties—even in the bar—where you can loudly celebrate without offending anyone.

Cloud Cliff Bakery-Cafe-Artspace

1805 Second Street. 983-6254.

Breakfast/ *Lunch:*	7 A.M.-.2 P.M. **Mon.-Fri.**
Brunch:	8 A.M.-2 P.M. **Sat-Sun.**
Bakery hours:	7 A.M.-6 P.M. **Mon.-Fri.**
Features:	**Beer/wine. Smoke-free. Patio. Free parking lot. Art.**
Price:	**Inexpensive. Visa/MasterCard.**
Cuisine:	**American.**

A big, easy room with lofty ceilings, high-tech lighting, lots of tables *and* a community table, a long bar for more seating facing an open grill, an espresso machine, a bakery that fills half the building (the aroma drives you wild), good local art on the walls, and a mighty-fine tradition of generous portions of homey food. All of this and you've got a very popular place to eat.

Mornings find Cloud Cliff bustling with locals and artists, but there's always room for one more.

Breakfast offers a wide selection from frittatas (Italian omelettes) to blue corn Amaranth pancakes, and vanilla French toast. Lunch emphasizes sandwiches made with their scrumptious breads.

The breads here are the best. The owners, Willem and Marion Malten, have spared no time or expense to get the greatest, organic flours from Kansas Menonite farmers to bake up an hon-est *Levain* loaf (whole wheat or white) along with countless other breads, rolls, muffins, cakes, pies, and cookies.

The Maltens dedication to fine art is a tradition here. Art openings are always well-attended by artists and friends; and the subsequent art shows continue to add visual interest for customers and staff.

Baja Tacos

2621 Cerrillos Road. 471-8762.

Breakfast/	
Lunch/Dinner:	7 A.M.-10 P.M. Mon.-Thurs.; 7 A.M.11 P.M. Fri. & Sat.; 8 A.M.-8 P.M. Sunday.
Features:	No alcohol. Catering available. Outside seating only. Free parking lot.
Price:	Budget. Major credit cards.
Cuisine:	New Mexican.

*H*ot 'n spicy—that's the way we like 'em. Tacos, that is. You might pass this one up if you didn't know locals love this place for its great green chile, oversized enchiladas, and fast food service.

There's even a happy hour from 5:30 to 6:30 P.M. when you can get a good deal on the already low prices.

Chicago Dog Express

---

600 Cerrillos Road. (Cerrillos and Paseo de Peralta). 984-2798.

Breakfast/	
Lunch:	8 A.M.-5 P.M. Mon.-Fri.; 10:30 A.M.-3 P.M. Sat. Closed Sunday.
Features:	No alcohol. Take-out. Outside seating only. Limited area deliveries. Free parking lot.
Price:	Budget. No credit cards.
Cuisine:	American.

*L*aid-back owner, Tom Fendley, and manager, Martin Gonzales, run this tiny take-out that bills itself as "Santa Fe's Best Hot Dog." Tom's been here since 1988 and draws a multi-cultural clientele.

The menu is short, down to business, and features *Vienna Pure Beef Hotdogs.*

All the dogs come regular or jumbo-sized, are "1/2 loaded" or "loaded," and slide into Vienna poppy seed buns.

Plain Dog with ketchup, mustard, relish, and onion starts out the menu and sets the basic ingredient standards for the other three.

Chicago Dog is the most ordered with additions of tomatoes, cucumbers, pickles, peppers, and celery salt. *The Coney Island* adds sauerkraut; and *Santa Fe Dog* has cheese and red or green chile. *Polish sausage* with 'kraut, mustard, and onions completes the meat picture.

For those not enamoured with beef, meatless *Frito Pies* come Jumbo or Monster-sized and excellent Posa's tamales are available.

Breakfast burritos can be delivered to your door from 8 A.M. to 10:30 A.M. If you're a kid thirteen and under or a senior citizen, you get special discounts on already cheap eats.

Horseman's Haven Cafe

6500 Cerrillos Road. 471-5420.

Breakfast/	
Lunch/Dinner:	8 A.M.-8 P.M. Mon.-Sat.; 8:30 A.M.-2 P.M. Sun.
Features:	No alcohol. Smoking. Free parking lot.
Price:	Budget. No credit cards.
Cuisine:	New Mexican.

No checks, no credit, no shirt, no shoes, no service. A lot of no's posted on the door that plainly lets you know where it's at. Horseman's Haven, almost eclipsed by the big Texaco gas station it sits beside, can be easily missed.

Located on the far, south side of Cerrillos Road, this tiny place is continuously packed with locals that hanker for Rose Romero's hot-hotter-hottest chile and the menu's low prices. The entire Romero family has run the Haven since 1981 and their presence is felt throughout: newspaper clips of wrestling matches abound on the walls saluting son, Rodney Romero; daughter, Kim, is busy waiting tables; Mr. Romero's behind the cafe's small bar still smoking cigarettes, pouring coffee, and ringing up the till; Mrs. Romero is in the kitchen cooking up her *Huevos Rancheros,* famous *Breakfast Burritos* or *Homemade Tortillas, Posole,* or *Blue Corn Enchiladas* and *Quesadillas.*

Nothing fancy about the Haven. But the Spanish music coming from a simple radio, little model horses sitting on the front windowsill, boots 'n saddle oilcloths on the tables, and the family busily keeping their customers happy—make this a *must do* for your eating itinerary.

Old Mexico Grill

✪

2434 Cerrillos Road.(Tucked in on southside of College Plaza South Shopping Center). 473-0338.

Lunch:	11:30 A.M.-2:30 P.M. Mon.-Fri.
Dinner:	5:30 P.M.-9 P.M. Sun.-Thurs.; 5:30 P.M.-9:30 P.M. Fri.-Sat.
Features:	Full Bar. Smoking/non-smoking. Free parking lot.
Price:	Moderate. Visa/MasterCard.
Cuisine:	Mexican.

*Y*ou won't find New Mexican food here. But you will find Old Mexican cuisine reflecting centuries of the indigenous dishes of Mexico. Don't let the shopping mall location put you off because, once inside, a trip to a south-of-the-border eat-fest is in order.

A comfortable bar with booths and a menu that offers seven different Margaritas, ten Mexican *cervezas* (beers), and bowls filled to the brim with addictive spicy-hot peanuts gladden the heart. There's an open grill in the main dining room so you can watch the flames leaping high as the cooks sizzle up your fajitas.

Favored dining room booths are a level up where you can watch all the activity. (Service can be inconsistent here, ranging from poor to very efficient and friendly.)

I can't come here and not order their *Caldo Tialpeno,* a Mexican chicken soup with chipotle chiles and vegetables that delivers deep, complex flavors. Traditional mole, a rich, dark, smooth sauce, with often up to twenty ingredients, including Mexican chocolate, is usually found on Mexican menus and here is no exception. *Mole Poblano de Guajolote* uses turkey breast (turkey is another key part of Mexican cooking) and is spicy with chiles.

Seafood is another important part of Mexico's cuisine so you'll find *Ceviche de Camarones y Conchas* on the menu, a Mexican classic—raw shrimp and scallops that cook in a marinade of lime juice, onions, peppers, and cilantro. Marinated and grilled meats and chicken with tortillas date back to early Indian civilizations and there's four different kinds. I always get the tasty *Tacos al Carbon,* either chicken or sirloin, or the excellent *Tacos de Cordero en Barbacoa,* shredded leg of lamb with ancho chile and mint barbeque sauce. *Arracheras,* pollo, carne, camarones, or vegetarian (also known in Texas as *fajitas*), are served sizzling hot on a platter with fresh tortillas. *Chipotle, tomatillo and avocado salsa* is divine.

 Mexican rice and black beans(refried or whole) accompany most of the house specials. Skip the familiar chile relleno and the fajitas and go for something a bit more exotic instead. Don't think for a minute that it's the same ol', same ol'—this food is robust—packed with flavor. The *Arroz con Leche y Chocolate Blanco,* custard rice pudding with raisins, cinnamon, nutmeg, and rum is first-rate.

The Pantry

1820 Cerrillos Road. 982-0179.

Breakfast/	
Lunch:	6:30 A.M.-2 P.M. Tues.-Sat.; 7:30 A.M.-2 P.M. Sun. Closed Monday.
Features:	No Alcohol. Smoking/non-smoking. Free parking lot.
Price:	Budget/Inexpensive. Visa/MasterCard.
Cuisine:	American/New Mexican.

*T*he Pantry could easily be the most displeasing-to-the-eye place to eat in Santa Fe—with its low-down, funky atmosphere, and clientele ranging from cops to suits to bikers to hairdressers to secretaries to housewives. Why, then, is the parking lot always packed, and the simple tables, original counter, and barstools filled with gratified bread-breakers?

 Could be an extensive breakfast menu with all items prepared fresh to order from the non-stop busy kitchen, and the happy-go-lucky waitresses who give astonishingly quick and efficient service to all. You can get eggs, steaks and chops, omelettes ("have it your way"), huge breakfast burritos with bacon, sausage, ham, chorizo or vegetarian; buttermilk and buckwheat pancakes; French toast; and waffles, traditional or Belgian, with pecans, blueberries, or strawberrries with or without whipped topping, and pure maple syrup for a $1.50 extra. The *Fresh Corned Beef* (Hash), one of The Pantry's specialties, can't be beat—and not a speck of grease. The corned beef is diced and sauteed with green onions, served on a bed of just-right home fries, and topped with two, perfect eggs—anyway you like 'em. Get the biscuits and gravy on the side. One of the best breakfast gravies I've had in years, it's thick, peppery, and filled with bits of sausage and bacon drippings. Yes, sir.

Ahhhh, fond memories of an old-fashioned luncheonette well up inside even the most hard-hearted diner, especially when you see the sandwiches sailing out of the kitchen atop the down-to-earth hands of waitress Lisa. There's a good-ol' Club with three decks of bacon, turkey, lettuce and tomato on toast; or the *New Mexican*, hot corned beef dripping with melted Swiss cheese and green chile, all bundled up in a flour tortilla. Of course there are hamburgers, New Mexican specialties (the combination plate is a good selection), bowls of green chile, chicken fried steak, pork chops, and a hot roast beef sandwich. All the sandwiches, steaks, and chops come with sides like French fries, biscuits, mashed potatoes, or vegetables.

It's such a good deal, money-wise, and the food is so comforting I guarantee you'll hear no whining from The Pantry's loyal customers—some coming here, I bet, since the place opened in 1947.

The "smile for today" part of the menu says it all: "Progress has been all right once, but it went on too long."

(Posa's) El Merendero

1945 Cerrillos Road. 820-7672.

Lunch/Dinner/	
Take Out:	8 A.M.-7 P.M. Mon-Sat. Closed Sunday.
Features:	No alcohol. Seating inside and out. Free parking lot.
Price:	Inexpensive. Major credit cards.
Cuisine:	New Mexican.

Second location: 907 West Alameda Street. 982-7672.

Breakfast/Lunch/	
Dinner/Take Out:	8:30 A.M.- 6 P.M. Mon.-Sat.; 9:30 A.M.-2:30 P.M. Sun.
Features:	No alcohol. Smoking. Free parking lot.

*M*ost Santa Feans know about (Posa's) El Merendero—you know, the take-out place on Siler Road? Well, that one is now wholesale only. But the good news is that the owners have opened up two retail outlets, one on Cerrillos Road in an

old drive-up burger joint and the other in Casa Solana, in a former fish restaurant. Not exactly strong on ambience, (Posa's) customers don't need or want it anyway. The strong suit here is their home-style *Tamales*—four different kinds— ordered up uno or by the dozen, hotter-than-hell posole and savory beans by the pint or gallon; the *Pico de Gallo Salsa* that guarantees to burn, and the *Tacos Al Pastor*—muy bueno.

Lots of folks order this simple, down-to-earth New Mexican food in large take-out quantities for all kinds of parties and get-togethers. And there's obviously a good reason why—lots of flavor.

Whether you're running around town and need to grab a fast lunch or you're ordering up for a big celebration, (Posa's) will please.

My favorite lunch is the *Tacos Al Pastor*, three, make-your-own soft tacos with bits of chewy, marinated sirloin (don't expect fork/butter-tender steak here, senor) with Pico de Gallo, beans, and lettuce—enough for two if you also get at least four of the *Green Chili* (their spelling) *Cheese Tamales* to go with. I dare you to try to resist the *Frito Pie*—one of those weird but essential New Mexican concoctions—Frito corn chips smothered with beans, (beef optional), red chile, lettuce, cheese, and onions.

Take along some breath mints if you are on your way to a meeting with your realtor!

Tecolote Cafe

★

1203 Cerrillos Road. 988-1362.

Breakfast/ Lunch:	7 A.M.-2 P.M. Tues.-Sun. Closed Monday.
Features:	No alcohol. Smoking/nonsmoking. Free parking lot.
Price:	Budget/Inexpensive. Major credit cards.
Cuisine:	New Mexican/American.

*T*his extremely popular place—especially with Santa Feans from all cultures— usually has a twenty to thirty-minute wait. But that doesn't phase the Tecolote Cafe's faithful of twenty years. It has been voted the "best breakfast" place many times in local newspapers and magazines, and has been featured in several national publications like Jane and Michael Stern's *Good Food/Road Food, Travel & Leisure* magazine, and *Money* magazine.

Why all the hub-bub? Stop in and try their *Huevos Rancheros, Green Chile Stew,* tender and syrup-soakable *Atole Piñon Hotcakes* with a side of bacon (my favorite), the bizarre *Chicken Livers Tecolote,* or *Fresh Asparagus & Hollandaise Eggs.*

Breakfast burritos, crispy, old fashioned pan-fried potatoes, and never-empty coffee cups (real half and half is served with the never-more-than-a-minute-old-coffee) are served in a simple, homey setting. Yellow and white-checked cafe curtains, a community table that ensures a no-wait situation if you're alone, and coat racks complete the picture.

Portions are generous, inexpensive, and the bakery basket that comes with most of the menu items is comforting and filled with their tender, homemade biscuits and blueberry muffins.

You get eight choices of fresh-baked breads for *French Toast* specials written on chalkboards in the three plain dining rooms: *Cinnamon Raisin, French, Molasses Oatmeal, Honey Wheat, Honey Almond Oat, Orange Poppyseed, Honey Blue Corn,* and *Honey Sesame.*

Everyone's friendly and the conversations roar in the early morning hours. Bring along a local daily paper to catch up on the news and join the cheerful energy.

Tortilla Flats

3139 Cerrillos Road. 471-8685.

Breakfast:	7 A.M.-5 P.M. daily.
Lunch:	11 A.M.-5 P.M. daily.
Dinner:	5 P.M.-10 P.M. daily.
Features:	Beer/Wine. Smoking/non-smoking. Free parking lot.
Price:	Inexpensive. Visa/MasterCard.
Cuisine:	American/New Mexican.

*E*ven though it may look like a "chain" from the outside, some of the New Mexican dishes are anything but chain-produced.

One favorite here is the *Vegetable Quesadilla* stuffed with fresh carrots, broccoli, and two cheeses (order the green chile on the side for dipping).

Another, the *Brisket Burrito,* served only after 5 P.M., is plump and meaty.

Don't overlook breakfast here with the likes of enchiladas, fajitas, sides of black beans, and blueberry pancakes.

Maria's New Mexican Kitchen

⭐

555 W. Cordova Road. 983-7929.

Lunch:	11 A.M.- 4 P.M. Mon.-Fri.; 12 P.M.-4 P.M. Sat.
Dinner:	5 P.M.-10 P.M. Mon.-Sat.; 12 P.M.-10 P.M. Sunday.
Features:	Full bar. Smoking/nonsmoking. Patio.
	Free parking lot. Art. [Historical]
Price:	Inexpensive. Major credit cards.
Cuisine:	New Mexican.

After trying dozens of different restaurants in Santa Fe, you will always come back to Maria's. Maria's remains a solid favorite with locals and visitors due to old Santa Fe landmark-ambience; a gigantic selection of tequilas, margaritas, and an authentic abundance of good, inexpensive New Mexican food.

Maria and Gilbert Lopez started a take-out kitchen in 1952 and continued to expand the building with used bricks from the old New Mexico State Penitentiary to build what is now called the restaurant's "Cantina". Also in the 50s, Santa Fe artist Alfred Morang (1901-1958) traded food for five wall frescos that still exist, respected and restored, on the Cantina's walls.

Another great showpiece in the Cantina is the bar's beer cooler—an 1881 icebox salvaged from the old mining town of Dawson, New Mexico. These kinds of historical touches and 40s re-creations are found throughout the newer additions to the original Cantina, thanks to more recent owners, Laurie and Al Lucero, who bought Maria's in 1985. Pre-World War II furniture from La Fonda Hotel, beams from the old PNM building in downtown Santa Fe, wide, rough wooden plank floors, hand-carved chairs and tables, lace cafe curtains, low ceilings, and three kiva fireplaces continue to keep the integrity of the original Maria's.

You can watch a woman making fresh tortillas behind a glass-walled room and hear soft guitar sounds from a strolling musician singing Spanish songs (at your request) while you peruse *Maria's Real Margarita* list. Drink decisions are tough, especially if you don't know about tequila—which I didn't until I asked our very capable and kind waitress for recommendations. She pointed out that ordering several different margaritas would give us a chance to sample different tequilas and thus find our favorite one. If you really want to get into it, try their tequila sampler: Choose any three tequilas, 1/2 ounce each, from group A, B, or C ($5 - $7.50) or different combinations from all three groups. Or order up the most expensive tequila ever made—100 percent Agave *Anejo Barrel Select Reserva de la Familia*—$4 a 1/2 ounce. (If you're now completely confused, read *Maria's Real Margarita Book*, Ten Speed Press, for everything you could want to know about tequila and Margaritas.) Anyway, we chose the house *Margarita*, *The Silver Herradura*, *The Grand Treasure*, and the *Margarita del Joven Esteban* (which won hands down for smooth, great taste).

The effort to keep the traditional, growing-up-in-Santa Fe-in-the-40s style intact may have you doing a double-take at the food prices. Most prices come in at $8 to $12 for an entree that could easily feed two. The most expensive item is the *Garlic-butter New York Steak* at $15.95 that's served with Spanish fries, Spanish onion rings (both are dipped in a chile batter and deep fried), and a salad.

At the $4.95 end of the menu is a bowl of *Green Chile Stew* that makes for a beggar's dinner but ends up making you feel like a rich person. With chunks of pork, potatoes, (beans, if you want, at no extra charge), and a sopaipilla or tortilla on the side, you'll know you've found one of the best bowls of green in Santa Fe. Order a side of sour cream to cool the palate—it's chile hot.

If you've never tried posole, a traditional Christmas season dish, order at least a cup. You'll either love or hate it. Maria's also offers lots of appetizers, sizzling fajitas, beef, chicken, or vegetarian; three other steaks and steak combo's; dinners of *Blue Corn Enchiladas, Tacos, Tostadas, Burrito Grande, Carne Adovada* (not for the faint-of-tongue), *Tamales, Rellenos,* and *Pork Spare Ribs* in a mild red chile barbeque sauce are part of a fifty-year-old tradition at Maria's.

Thank goodness there's a child's plate of tacos, or cheese enchiladas and a burrito that can be ordered without chile or light chile.

Finish off your meal with a decent *Flan*—real burnt-sugar caramel sauce pooled around a creamy smooth custard.

Marisco's "La Playa"

537 Cordova Road. 982-2790.

Lunch/Dinner: 11 A.M.-9 P.M. Mon.; 11 A.M.-11 P.M. Wed. & Thurs.;
10 A.M.-11 P.M. Fri.; 10 A.M.-10 P.M. Sat. & Sun.
Closed Tuesday.
Features: Beer. Smoking. Free parking lot.
Price: Inexpensive/Moderate. Visa/MasterCard.
Cuisine: Mexican seafood.

*Q*uite a different—but heartily welcome—addition to Santa Fe's eating scene is this funny little joint—a family-owned Mexican seafood restaurant that has the word "SEA*FOOD" painted in big letters across their plate glass window that looks out over an ordinary parking lot. Owners, Jose Ortega, and his cousin, Luis Ortega, both originally from Chihauhau, Mexico (and former plasterers here in Santa Fe) have employed cooks from Puerto Vallarta and created a very authentic south-of-the-border seafood eatery.

The decor is turquoise formica, and the room is simple and small. There's one waitress and two cooks, so don't expect any frills or fuss here. What you can expect however is an extensive menu in Spanish and English featuring *only* seafood—from *caldos* (soups) to *tacos de pescado o camaron* (fish or shrimp tacos) to *camarones maneados* (shrimp rolled with bacon and Mexican cheese) to *pescado sarandeado* (a 10-ounce fried trout marinated in garlic sauce to *ostiones en su 1/2 concha* (fresh gulf oysters on the half-shell). There is one meat dish, the *filete a la plancha*, a good size filet seasoned and marinated and then broiled, and served with coast sauce.

Prices may seem high for lunchtime, but when you see the size of the portions (grande) and realize that shrimp and other seafood is not an inexpensive item, you'll cool out. *Vuelvea la vida* or the "comeback-to-life seafood combo" soup comes in a bowl the size of a large mixing bowl. I watched several young people happily slurpping it up for lunch. And I realized that two could easily share it for lunch and four people could share it as a first course.

The clear broth base has plenty of carrots, celery, and onions and is swimming with shrimps, octopus, scallops, crab, and oysters. Just pick up the crab leg and twist out the meat, neat!

The paprika-coated French fries that come with the "specialities" are redeemable once you dip them in the remarkable avocado-cream-jalapeño-tomato-sauce/

onion dip (I've never had anything like it and ended up eating it with a spoon) that arrives at your table before you can say *sabrosa*, along with a basket of corn chips and a fiery hot jalapeño-cilantro-onion salsa. (On a scale of 1 to 10 with 10 being the hottest, it's a 10.) If that's still not hot enough for you, there are three bottled salsas with Mexican labels on each table for extra paralizing heat.

The rice is seasoned with green, red, and yellow diced peppers and is simply delicious. The *Shrimp Cocktail* is easily a meal: It's served in a large, old fashioned glass ice cream sundae dish and becomes a shrimp "sundae" layered with lots of plump shrimp, onions, cilantro, tomatoes, juiced up with Clamato. These kind of cocktails are standard fare in Mexico, but become an unusual treat in New Mexico.

There's still a lot of other goodies on the menu, not to mention a menu *para los niños* (for the kids) that offers smaller portions of tacos, a burrito, quesadilla, and a hamburger with Mexican cheese.

Pyramid Cafe

⊗

505 Cordova Road. 989-1378.

Lunch/Dinner: 11:00 A.M.-8:00 P.M. Mon.-Thurs.; 11:00 A.M.-9:00 P.M
          Fri.-Sat. Closed Sunday.
Features: No alcohol. Smoke-free.
Price: Budget/Inexpensive. No credit cards.
Cuisine: Greek/Mediterranean.

I love these kinds of places—zero frills, low prices, generous portions, bustling kitchen. You can come in wearing shorts and thongs and fit right in with the youthful crowd that eats healthy fare here for less money. Order at the counter from the menu or boards posted above.

The Gyro meats here are spit-roasted in the traditional, vertical way and the end result is that unforgettable, fabulous taste that's always associated with the Greek gyro sandwich. The Pyramid piles the lamb (chunked rather than sliced) on a huge pita along with lettuce, onion, tomato, and tzatziki sauce—I could barely get my hands around it much less my mouth, but I persevered and won. Delicious.

And if you don't like lamb, you can get a chicken gyro. The house specialty is the *Pyramid Pinnacle Platter*—grilled lamb and a chicken kabob served over basmati rice topped with house-made marinara sauce, Greek salad on the side. All for $6.95.

Vegetarians rejoice! You get lots of choices on this menu: falafel sandwiches and platters, moussaka, spanakopita, tyropita, humous, tabouleh, baba ganouj, and dolmas.

Carry-out is also available.

Chow's

720 St. Michael's Drive. 471-7120.

Lunch:	11:30 A.M.-2 P.M. Mon.-Fri.; 12 P.M.-3 P.M.-Sat.
Dinner:	5 P.M.-9 P.M. Mon.-Sat. Closed Sunday.
Features:	Beer/Wine. Smoke-free. Banquet room.
	Outside seating. Free parking lot.
Price:	Inexpensive. Major credit cards.
Cuisine:	Chinese.

*I*mplanted in a shopping center, Chow's charming owners offer a calm retreat from the busy streets. It's like California meets Chinatown meets New Mexico—and the result is clean, light, no-MSG, contemporary, eclectic Chinese cuisine.

Appetizers seem to work the best. There's *Firecracker Dumplings:* steamed dim sum pastry stuffed with carrots, onions, chicken; and *Chile* served with Chinese pesto spinach sauce; or *Ranch Spring Rolls*—crispy crunchies filled with cabbage, carrots, green onions; and *Chicken* with an excellent orange ginger glaze; and *Chow's Baby Back BBQ Ribs*—glistening ruby-sauced tidbits without the slighest hint of grease.

Order individually or ask for the *Assorted Pleasures*—a sampler of the appetizers—or order the sampler as your main meal. Noodle dishes are huge and satisfying. But the *Won-ton Soup* can be flavorless and some of the main dishes lack the complex flavors you've come to expect in Chinese cooking.

Lucy's Dark Chocolate-dipped fortune cookies are an unusual twist to an old favorite. Or wait for the regular ones that always come at the end of the meal.

Felipe's Tacos

1711 Llano Street A. (In St. Michael's Village.) 473-9397.

Breakfast: 9 A.M.-11 A.M. Saturday only.
Lunch: 10:30 A.M.-7 P.M. Mon.-Fri; 9 a.m.-4 P.M. Sat.
    Closed Sunday.
Features: No alcohol. Smoke-free. Outside seating.
    Free parking lot.
Price: Inexpensive. No credit cards.
Cuisine: Mexican.

*F*elipe is from California, and his mother and her heirloom recipes are from Zacatecas, Mexico. Together, they have created a real *taqueria* right in the center of Santa Fe, in a plain shopping center.

Felipe's has a health-conscious attitude: Lean steaks and skinless chickens are grilled, no lard is used, beans and rice are cooked up fresh, salsas are prepared daily, and there's a lot of vegetarian dishes.

Soft Tacos (the way you get 'em in Mexico), *Quesadillas, Burritos, Tortas, Combinaciones,* and *A la cartas*—are all available vegetarian.

Once you pick up the order you placed at the counter, skoot over to the salsa bar and add red and/or green chile salsas, fresh Pico de Gallo, lime, radishes, chopped onion, and fresh cilantro to your plate for added authenticity and just the right mix of flavors to complement the food.

Felipe's can be very busy during lunch catering to nearby businesses and students from the College of Santa Fe. But jump right in line and get their tasty tacos to eat in or take out.

Green Onion Sports Pub and Restaurant

1851 St. Michaels Drive. 983-5198.

Lunch/Dinner: 11 A.M.-9:30 P.M. daily.
Full bar: Open until 2 A.M. Mon.-Sat. and until midnight Sun.
Features: Smoking. Free parking lot.
Seniors age sixty or over—10 percent discount.
Price: Inexpensive. Major credit cards.
Cuisine: American/New Mexican.

This local-packed Irish sports bar attracts unlikely combinations: art dealers, politicians, writers, homeboys, secretaries, and real estate folks, young and old. They all come for the generous portions of pub food such as basic or super *Half-pounder Burgers* with curly, seasoned fries or jumbo *Beer-Batter Onion Rings.* Or the big, big portions of New Mexican specialties: *Burritos, Frito pies, Carne Adovada, Fajitas, Green Chile Stew,* and *Chile Rellenos;* or daily specials like *Pork Roast and Mashed Potatoes;* or hefty sandwiches like the popular *Home Plate: The Shamrock,* a Philly steak sandwich with a New Mexican twist (green chile strips).

And there's pizza, too. This can all be washed down with an ice cold beer or iced tea served by friendly, T-shirted young waitresses ("What do you want to drink, Sweetie?").

Lots of fun appetizers like *Buffalo Wings, nachos,* plain or supreme, a *Quesadilla, Pepper Poppers,* (breaded red peppers stuffed with cream cheese), and *Carne Guisada* (pork cooked in herbs and spices with Pico de Gallo, sour cream and flour tortillas on the side) can be pinch-hitters for your main meal while watching the major leagues on TV.

Sports fans come to cheer their teams on with the help of ten satellite televisions, stragically placed around two main rooms for easy viewing from the long bar or dining tables. Dozens of team banners are plastered to the ceiling in the bar area; the NFL schedule for the week is posted, and walls display framed caricature drawings of their customers. Smaller video screens are nearby so your table can play Jeopardy-type, interactive trivia games while chowing down.

Dark, noisy, smokey, and very down-to-earth—The Green Onion is an interesting alternative to more well-known and expensive downtown restaurants. Look for the big neon shamrock that sits in the satellite dish out front and come on St. Patrick's Day—join the madness.

Mucho: The Gourmet Sandwich Shoppe

1711 Llano Road (G.) 473-7703.

Lunch:	10:30 A.M.-3 P.M. Mon.-Fri.
Features:	No alcohol. Smoke-free. Outside seating.
	Free parking lot. Free delivery to limited areas
	11 A.M.-2:30 P.M. Mon.-Fri.
Price:	Inexpensive. Major credit cards.
Cuisine:	American.

*T*his is the original Mucho. There's another one downtown on Palace Street, and they both do well catering to local businesses. For the lunch crowd there are over twenty sandwiches on the menu with new ones posted daily on a board. The sandwiches are original and outrageous—above and beyond the ordinary.

There are salads: *Chef's, Tuna, Chicken, Avocado,* and *Garden*—all served on a bed of gourmet garden greens topped with avocado, cucumber, tomato, and croutons. Ranch, Thousand Island, Bleu Cheese, or light vinaigrette are dressing choices. Deli-sides of salads like potato, pasta, and coleslaw are made fresh daily.

Since sandwiches are the big deal here, let's get to it. Some of the more unusual ones include the *Mucho Meatball Sub* with spicy meatballs smothered with Provolone cheese and special Mucho sauce served on an eight-inch sub-roll. *Prime Delight,* prime beef, cream cheese, tomato, sweet onions, mayo, horserad-ish, and lettuce comes on the same sub-roll. Get this, the new *Spinach and Egg Classic* with fresh egg salad, bacon, spinach, tomato, blue cheese dressing on multi-grain bread provides a salad/sandwich combo for those who like it all together.

Classic sandwiches are not ignored here, just pumped up a bit with more goodies. The *Rueben Deluxe* has more of everything and the *Santa Fe Cheese Steak* adds green chiles. There's a *Turkey Melt, The Veggie, Almond Albacore Tuna, BBQ Beef,* and a *New Mexico BLT* with cream cheese and avocado.

Everything on the menu (except the Reuben) is under $5 (includes tax) making this a great bargain in a city that tends to be pricey. It doesn't matter that there's no ambience or atmosphere—because there's also no pinching of the pocketbook.

Castro's Comidas Nativas Restaurante

997 Rodeo Road at Richard's Avenue. 438-0146.

Lunch/Dinner: 11 A.M.-9 P.M. Mon.-Sat. Closed Sun.
Features: No alcohol. Smoke-free. Free parking lot.
Price: Inexpensive. Major credit cards.
Cuisine: New Mexican.

A bona fide New Mexican restaurant on the not-so-glamorous side of town that goes about the business of serving generous portions of inexpensive classics like enchiladas, tamales, huevos rancheros, chalupas, chile rellenos, menudo, and posole.

The interior is all formica with lots of Virgin of Guadalupe renderings on the walls and a crucifix hanging over the arch that connects the two dining rooms. When was the last time you saw someone saying grace over their meal in a restaurant? I saw it here. That's the kind of place it is. Simple, honest, local, family-run.

The priciest item on the menu is the ten-ounce *New Mexican Steak* served with an enchilada, rice, posole, and a sopaipilla—all for $8.99. Everything else generally falls into the $4.75 to $5.75 category and below.

Castro's red and green chiles are really good. The pleasing red was not too hot and had the color of an old brick—deep burgundy. Daily specials are written on a board and could be *Chicken Fajitas.* Just to give you an idea of what I mean by generosity here, the fajitas consist of a plate of good-sized strips of marinated chicken—white meat only—out-numbering the sauteed peppers and onions. Good, not-too-cheesy refried beans, seasoned rice, ramekins of red and green chile, and a large, hot-off-the-griddle tortilla are served on the side.

A nice surprise is that there is only one menu all day, and the prices don't change.

The Bishop's Lodge

Bishop's Lodge Road, Tesuque. 983-6377.

Brunch:	11 A.M.-2 P.M. Sundays.
Breakfast:	7:30 A.M.-10 A.M. daily.
Lunch:	11:30 A.M.-2 P.M. Mon.-Sat.
Dinner:	6 P.M.-9 P.M. daily.
Features:	Full BAR. Smoke-free. Smoking permitted on patio. Free parking lot. Art. [Historical]
Price:	Moderate/Expensive. Major credit cards.
Cuisine:	American.

*A*mericans are still wild about Sunday brunch. And to prove it, The Bishop's Lodge offers a stunning brunch buffet every Sunday that always attracts a full house of guests and locals alike.

This resort sits in the foothills of the Sangre de Christo mountains on a thousand acres of rolling green hills—so it's not a bad idea to take one their nature walks or a horseback ride into some scenic meadow before plunging into their renowned brunch. If nothing else, you'll feel less guilty later on about going over your allotment of fat grams. If walking's not enough there *is* an exercise room and tennis court for guests. If you're not staying at the Lodge, the short drive north on old Bishop's Lodge Road to Tesuque is magnificent.

There is only a small sign indicating where you turn into Bishop's Lodge, so be alert. There's a little bit of a climb to the main building from the lower parking lots. Keep that in mind if you have elderly or handicapped passengers and drive on up to the main entrance to leave them, breathing intact. Be sure to spend a bit of time in the main Lodge's grand sitting room complete with gigantic fireplace and Indian textiles on the walls before starting brunch.

Once you catch sight of the buffet tables there will be no holding you back. I recommend that you make reservations for an early hour—say 11:30 A.M.—simply because the food is untouched and arranged beautifully. The front table gets you started and is virtually groaning with salads, breads, fruits, deviled eggs, hams, cheeses, and a poached salmon waiting to be dressed up with capers and dill sauce. There's also Nova, cream cheese, and chopped onion to go on one of the many bagels; *and* prosciutto and melon. Caution! I could have made a meal here without going any further, but there's lots more.

(Remember, you don't have to load up on your first go-'round—pace it out.)

Take a moment and gaze out at the cottonwood trees shading the terraces (in summer) that flank the inside dining rooms—and sip fresh coffee that is being replenished about every two seconds by gaggles of speedy servers. One server was actually startled when I said "stop" to the tenth refill. Because buffet dishes can be rather mystifying, there are placecards in front of each dish identifying them, in case you can't.

Unless you like your egg yolks cooked hard-boiled, pass up the *Eggs Benedict* which suffer from a long sit in the steam server (maybe the Lodge can figure out a better way to serve these brunch favorites.)

Definitely get the *Chicken Breasts* stuffed with chorizo, a hot, spicy sausage, the *Roast Pork Loin* with apple-cranberry relish, and the *Roast Beef,* sliced to order with au jus and horseradish sauce. The *Roasted, Baby Potatoes* and fresh julienne vegetables keep you guilt-free—at least for the moment—and the *Cheese Blinztes* with fruit sauce, *Chile Rellenos, Baked Marlin* and rice add extra pizzazz

The desserts waiting on another large table might as well have Bruce Nauman's avaricious neon mounted above them flashing a stern warning about gluttony. Brush all those thoughts away and move on into dangerous territory: Chocolate cake, carrot cake, apple and pumpkin pies, bread pudding, English trifle, coconut-raspberry pudding, cream puffs, napoleans, cannolis stuffed with nuts and cream and dipped in chocolate. Ditto for the fresh strawberries, and custard filled raspberry tarts the size of silver dollars that confirm what your conscience suspected.

Pay the bill, waddle outside, and reconsider taking the aforementioned walk, if you haven't already.

Tesuque Village Market & Bakery

Highway 285 North to Tesuque, exit to Highway 591. 988-8848.

Breakfast/	
Lunch/Dinner:	6 a.m.-10 p.m. daily.
Features:	Beer/wine. Smoke-free. Patio.
	Smoking permitted on patio.
	Free parking lot. [Historical]
Price:	Budget/Inexpensive. Major credit cards.
Cuisine:	American/New Mexican.

*W*hen what must be one of the most beautiful Flea Markets in the world opens its gates to eager fleaers in the spring, Tesuque Village Market begins to hum. The deal is: One must start out early for the Flea Saturday or Sunday morning, score some great jewelry or any one of a thousand treasures offered here and, then, worn out and hungry, head for the Market.

This has been considered a time-honored tradition, if not a legendary act, in and around Santa Fe. Why, you ask? Because, in the past, there was a feeling of old-fashioned camaraderie and community spirit. The food was good and the service friendly.

The Market, however, has definitely made changes since it first opened, causing Santa Feans and Tesuque residents to raise their culinary eyebrows. New management claims the changes have been necessary to accommodate larger crowds. The result? The quality of food and consistency of service has suffered.

Even so, it's worth the risk to at least have breakfast here after the flea market. And, if you're lucky, the *Blueberry Buttermilk Pancake* (one cake is the size of a dinner plate) with real maple syrup and a side of bacon will be as fine as I've had it in the past.

Grab a loaf of their *Green Chile/Cheese Bread* (it has been the best of its kind), a dozen *calabacitos tamales* (squash), *homemade potato salad,* a souvenir map, a Tesuque Village T-shirt, a *New York Times,* and anything else that calls to you as you walk out to your car.

Leona's de Chimayó

At El Santuario de Chimayó, Chimayó. 351-4569.

Hours:	Open daily or when the Santuario is open.
Features:	No alcohol.Take-out. Mail order: 1-800-4-LEONAS.
	Free parking lot. [Historical]
Price:	Budget. No credit cards.
Cuisine:	New Mexican.

*W*hen I met Father Roca inside his ancient parish, El Santuario de Chimayó, he told me that he has known Leona Tiede since she was a girl. Father Roca came from Barcelona, Spain, years ago to preside over the Santuario and now claims he is but one of the rocks (Roca) that belongs to the mountains. For seventeen years, Leona was known mostly for her freshly baked tortillas which were sold at an open-air restaurant-stand on Highway 76 near Chimayó. Even though she hand-made 36-dozen tortillas every morning, she always sold out by day's end.

Leona's tireless energy led her to develop the now-famous flavored tortillas that are shipped all over the world. Sweet varieties include raspberry, pineapple, amaretto, apple-cinnamon, and Jamaican rum—savory tortillas might be garlic, piñon, spicy jalapeño, and Cheddar cheese—all packed by the dozen. The surprise is that Leona (married twenty-nine years, and a grandmother) has opened another roadside restaurant—this time in the parking lot of the Santuario—due to the encouragement of long-time friend, Father Roca.

Her biggest day falls on Good Friday when she sets up an assembly-line take-out for the thousands of hungry pilgrims who arrive at the Santurario for Lent. At this time Leona rolls out burritos, tacos, and tamales for the faithful.

The word is out about Leona's and folks from all over come here, summer and winter. East coast tourists are startled when they see the *Polish Sausage Burrito* on Leona's small menu. Leona's eyes light up and she just chuckles. Excellent red and green chile is made fresh daily and she prides herself on the fact that only garlic and water is added to her chile sauces. Calabasitas (squash) or pork and cheese is tucked into Leona's fat *Tamales*—all handmade. (I found out that these are the same tamales served at neighboring Rancho de Chimayó Restaurante.

Biscochitos (small anise seed cookies, usually made on holidays) are so in demand that Leona has a hard time keeping up with the orders. Other items to get are the *Frito Pie*, bowls of *posole, beans,* or *menudo. Panocha,* a sprouted wheat

◆ *chímayó*

Lent pudding, is hard to find—so get it here.

There are some stone stools and tables available if you want to sit down for your hand-held meal. Get a dozen tamales and chile to take home. Leona happily packs it up for you and if you're lucky, she might tell you her favorite way to prepare them.

Restaurante Rancho de Chimayó

County Road 98 (Scenic high road to Taos), Chimayó.
351-4444 or 984-2100.

Breakfast:	8:30 A.M.-10:30 A.M. Sat. & Sun.
Lunch:	11:30 A.M.-3:30 P.M. Mon.-Fri.;
	11 A.M.-3:30 p.m. Sat. & Sun.
Dinner:	4 P.M.-9 P.M. daily. Closed Monday in Winter.
Features:	Full bar. Smoke-free dining rooms. Smoking in bar.
	Patio. Free parking lot. [Historical]
Price:	Inexpensive/Moderate. Major credit cards.
Cuisine:	New Mexican.

*T*he Jaramillo family had a vision of preserving their historical heritage back in 1965, and Restaurante Rancho de Chimayó now stands proudly nestled beneath the Sangre de Cristo Mountains as a homage to their extraordinary foresight. The Jaramillos can trace their beginnings in New Mexico to ancestors, Jose Jaramillo Negrete and wife Maria de Sotomayor, who came here as colonists from Mexico City in 1693. (We are talking roots, here.)

The Jaramillos' love of the land shows in the care they have given to the buildings, plants, trees, and apple orchard that spreads out before the restaurant. Recently, the Jaramillo family completed restoration of another family property (across the highway) and created Hacienda Rancho de Chimayó, an inn with seven guest rooms, each with private enclosed courtyards, sitting areas, fireplaces, antiques, and private baths.

The drive to Chimayó is splendid. Don't even think of rushing this one. Take time to drink in the history and beauty of the area. Most know that Rancho de Chimayó's neighbor, tiny El Santuario de Chimayó or The Shrine of Chimayó, is the first order of the day before lunch or dinner. (Approximately 300,000 visitors a year come to The Shrine that is now a National Historic Landmark.)

A cascading waterfall of large ruby-red ristras dripping from the building's eaves and a bronze statue of San Francisco de Asis (Asisi) greet you as you approach the front door of Rancho de Chimayó Restaurante. Inside, just off to the left of the waiting area, are two small adobe rooms left from the original homestead. Fireplaces add a warm glow to these dining areas and vintage photographs that line the walls keep you in touch with the family's history. Notice the framed wedding invitation dating back to November 26, 1906, announcing an ancestral marriage. There are shrines and candles, and pictures of saints throughout—all set against white-washed adobe walls.

Towards the back of the restaurant is the popular covered patio room with rows of French doors that allow diners to look outside at the three-tiered patio. In summer, these doors are flung open to let in the glorious air. A real treat is the Cantina, where a double shepard's fireplace takes center attention. The space in the bar area has lots of old-paned windows, the uneven floors are dark, with wide-planked wood, the chairs low and comfy, the drinks refreshing and colorful. Bright red-pink *Chimayó Cocktails* (Jose Cuervo Gold tequila, Creme de Cassis, and apple cider) come from the bar to the dining rooms with amazing regularity.

A good appetizer to go with your cocktail are the *Stuffed Jalapeños*—grease-free, crunchy little deep-fired bullets of jalapeños, black beans, and Monterey Jack cheese. A mild, tomatoey salsa is nearby for dipping. A good *Tortilla Soup* should have a successful balance between texture and flavor. Rancho de Chimayó's soup succeeds with chunks of chicken, crispy strips of tortilla chips, spicy broth, avocado, cilantro, and cheeses.

Lunch and dinner menus are basically identical except there are no a la carte selections at dinner. Sixteen comidas nativas (native dishes) head the entrees. Their *Stacked Enchiladas* (order Christmas chile) keep competition stiff; and the *Carne Adovada Burrito,* a good sixteen inches long, is stuffed with chile-infused brisket meat, wrapped in a flour tortilla, and topped with avocado sauce and melted cheeses. Refried beans on the side. Rancho de Chimayó's green chile is soupy and slightly thickened with starch. The two sopaipillas that come with all entrees are not as delectable as others I've had. But you couldn't ask for nicer waitresses.

Save room for *Natillas* (vanilla pudding that's more like a thin custard reminiscent of a French floating island) dolloped with real whipped cream or a well-above-average flan. Both give a cool end to a spicy meal.

On the way out you may want to check out their showroom of collectibles and art of the Southwest that is presided over by a great grandson of the family.

Embudo Station

1101 Drive, Highway 68. (41 miles north of Santa Fe.) 852-4707.

Lunch/Dinner:	12 p.m.-9 p.m. Tues.-Sun. Closed Monday. Only open April through October.
Features:	Beer/wine. Smoke-free. Smoking permitted on patio. Free parking lot. [Historical]
Price:	Inexpensive/Moderate. Major credit cards.
Cuisine:	American/Barbeque.

*E*mbudo Station, population twenty one, is still a popular destination for many a barbeque-beer pilgrim—especially since this piece of paradise practically sits in the Rio Grande River. The restaurant, that shares the same name and location as the tiny town, smokes its own meats, river trout, hams, turkeys, and game hens, and serves them up to hoardes of hungry visitors—along with their own micro-brewed, red or green chile beers: The *Rio Grande Green,* a golden ale fermented with green chiles and the *Ristra,* a red ale fermented with red chiles, were both gold medal winners at the New Mexico State Fair in 1994.

It's not just the smoked delicacies and beers that brings 'em coming—it's the entire experience. Take a leisurely drive from Santa Fe up through the southern part of the Rio Grande Gorge in September or October, stop in Velarde for delicious New Mexican apples, or drop by the many fruit stands along the way. Finally, on the restaurant's outdoor patio (really, the only place to sit) under giant, ancient cottonwoods, watch the Rio Grande slide by while sipping on that beer; run for cover when the occasional thunderstorm builds to a very wet downpour; or maybe stroll up the river bank for a brief moment of contemplation and skip a stone across the narrow waters—all part of the perfect "American Sunday Drive."

There's jazz on the weekends, a place to sign up for their fall catalog of smokehouse meats that are shipped fresh to your door by UPS or 2nd day air. There are no-whitewater, "dinner" raft floats for the mildly adventurous, and an art gallery/gift shop for those who can't stop buying souvenirs.

The food itself may be secondary to the experience, but it satisfies that urge for an outdoor, picnic-like meal.

Lunch and dinner have basically the same menu except that dinner costs more. Stick to the Smokehouse platters like the *Smokehouse Rib Platter* with baby back pork ribs or the *Smokehouse Lunch Specialty,* oak smoked trout. The *Barbequed Brisket Sandwich* and the *Cold Smoked Turkey Sandwich* are popular and taste even better with one of Embudo Station's cold, chile beers.

Gabriel's

US 285 (12 miles north of Santa Fe). 455-7000.

Lunch/Dinner:	**11:30 A.M.-9:30 P.M. Sun.-Thurs. & 11:30 A.M.-10 P.M. Fri.& Sat.**
Features:	**Full bar. Smoking/nonsmoking. Patio. Free parking lot.**
Price:	**Inexpensive-Moderate. Major credit cards.**
Cuisine:	**New Mexican.**

*T*here are two things you must do on arrival: Order ice-cold Margaritas with salt and the *Guacamole* prepared table-side. Now, sit back, sip your drink and watch your guacamole be prepared, Oaxacan-style, in a large stone *metate*. On the cart with the avocados and the metate are small dishes filled with fresh chopped garlic, onions, cilantro, salt, lime juice, tomatoes, and jalapeño chiles that will be added, as per your instructions, to the chopped avocados. Tell the waiter you want everything in it! This is, by far, one of the best guacamoles you'll get in New Mexico. It's served with a basket of crunchy tortilla chips and some excellent salsa fresca (fresh tomatoes, onions, garlic, jalapeño chiles, cilantro), and will feed four easily as an appetizer, or two as a meal.

Don't balk at the $7.95 price tag—it's well worth it. There is a large selection of other New Mexican and Old Mexico dishes to choose from that are also good: Try the *Plato de Carnitas* with tortillas and all the trimmings to make your own fresh, soft tacos.

Bobcat Bite Restaurant

Old Las Vegas Highway South. (Bobcat Ranch) 983-5319.

Lunch/Dinner:	11 A.M.-7:50 P.M. Wed.-Sat. Closed Sun., Mon. & Tues.
Features:	No alcohol. Smoking. Free parking lot. [Historical]
Price:	Budget/Inexpensive. No credit cards.
Cuisine:	American.

*P*ull in when you see the neon bobcat sign above a small, low-slung building with a parking lot full of potholes and four-wheelers. This is one of those road eateries that is forever locked into a space-time warp. And lucky for us.

Owner, Rene Clayton, has been smoothly running Bobcat for fifteen years and told us that the restaurant has been in operation for over forty years. The success of this shoe-box-of-a-restaurant is in its no-frills simplicity—generous heapings of food, stripped-down decor, competent quick service, and low, low prices. It also appeals to Americana's homespun dreams of an earlier, easier time, when cowhands wrangled and ate a lot of beef. (You can almost hear the horses snorting at the hitching posts outside.)

Notice that there are written rules to be obeyed if you want to keep everything shipshape and orderly (necessary, considering the space). First, a list posted just outside the door as you enter explains seating, waiting, and other important matters. Once seated at one of the five tables or nine seats at the counter made out of logs (twenty-four seats in all), the menu (same for lunch and dinner) will instruct you about paying and inform you how to order your beef—rare to well.

The *13-ounce Ribeye Steak* is juicy and flavorful and comes with hashbrowns or potato salad; tossed iceberg lettuce salad or cole slaw and garlic bread. There's also *Pork Chops,* a *12-ounce Ham Steak,* a *13-ounce Hamburger Steak,* a *Ribeye and Salad platter,* side orders of the above salads, hashbrowns, chile bowl (winter only), and green chile.

The big favorite here is the top-flight *Green Chile Cheeseburger,* sizing in at an inch-and-a-half thick. The burger is topped with a nice melted square of American white Swiss. Green chile is slathered over all, and it's served up on a toasted bun. After this burger experience you will know that Bobcat Bite serves the best burger in Santa Fe County. (I suggest you order it medium-rare to medium for the juice-down-the-elbow effect.) Besides two other burgers, a grilled cheese, a grilled ham and cheese, and a ham, that's about it.

No dessert, no fancy sczhmancy—and no one ever leaves Bobcat Bite unhappy.

Dim Sum—Then Some Restaurant

State Road 14 (Turquoise Trail) at County Road 45. 474-4111

Dim Sum:	11 A.M.-8 P.M. Saturday & 9:30 A.M.-3:30 P.M. Sun.
Dinner:	5 P.M.-8 P.M. Saturday only.
Features:	No alcohol. Smoking-non-smoking. Patio.
	Catering available. Free parking lot.
Price:	Budget/Moderate. Visa/MasterCard.
Cuisine:	Chinese.

*I*f you have no idea what dim sum is, you've missed out on what a large part of the world's population has enjoyed for thousands of years. Dim sum means, in Cantonese, "to dot the heart," also known in Mandarin as *tien hsin* or "the heart-touchers."

In food talk these Chinese bite-size delicacies form a huge category of steamed, baked, and deep fried dumplings filled with meat and/or vegetables, and also include dishes of duck's feet (with the webs of course), spicy, wide rice noodles, spareribs, and on and on.

Dim sum varieties can number in the hundreds at the big, bustling dim sum parlors in San Francisco and New York where the little "dishes of the heart" are wheeled around on stainless steel carts by uniformed servers to hundreds of customers eagerly pointing to the little dishes of their choice.

On any given day in Chinatown, U.S.A., families and friends traditionally gather at large round tables with the-ever-so-convenient lazy susan strategically placed in the center for easy reach. Amid the sounds of chop sticks clicking and high-pitched conversation, pots and pots of jasmine tea are consumed to wash down the dim sum.

So how on earth did a dim sum restaurant end up in New Mexico you say?— through the dreams and determination of owner Mimi Ho. Mimi was born in Shanghai in the 30s, endured part of the beginnings of World War II in Hong Kong, and immigrated with her family to America in 1939. In August of 1993, with a world of experience behind her, she opened her restaurant. Since then, every weekend, her dim sum has been rolling out of the kitchen pleasing Santa Fe with a surprisingly wide assortment of *Dumplings, Jasmine* and *Chrysanthemum teas, Peking Duck* and *Lobster Cantonese* (order two days in advance), and a dinner menu that also includes dim sum.

This place is out in the middle of nowhere (almost), past the state prison, and housed in a modest building with plenty of dirt-lot parking. Inside, knotty pine walls, plank wood floors, chalk boards displaying dim sum and other special Chinese dishes, globe lanterns, a lone Chinese figurine on one of the mantels shared with a two-sided fireplace, and a row of soft drink cans on the other, tell it like it is.

Once you get the hang of dim sum you'll find out that you don't have to gobble up the first offerings out of Mimi's spotlessly clean kitchen. Take your time. Think of this meal as a two hour event, at least. Sample, nibble, drink your

tea. Socialize. Relax.

Now, get your chopsticks into position—here it comes in a seemingly endless stream of bite-size goodies with names like *cha su pow, sumai, har gaw, bao, sao fun,* and *jia tse: Cold Sesame Noodles* in little bowls, *Cucumber Salad* in a spicy vinaigrette, *Spareribs, Dumplings* with mushroom or curried chicken fillings, juicy and tender *Chicken Teryiaki Drumsticks, Steamed Shrimp Dumplings,* very crispy *Wontons, Spring Rolls,* melt-in-your-mouth *Shrimp Toast, Armenian Cucumber* stuffed with garden-fresh vegetables (Mimi has her own garden), and meats in the shape and texture of a cylindrical meatloaf, *Cantonese Chicken,* wide *Rice Noodles in Broth, Schezwan Shrimp* and *Calamari* with rice and mushrooms, and their house specialty, *Daikon Cakes* (shredded daikon radish combined with sticky rice and deep fried).

Be prepared—just when you think you can't pop another dim sum into your mouth, more selections continue to tempt you, especially if the place is crowded—more folks equal more dim sum.

Desserts are curiously American. The traditional flaky, tender custard tarts or the sweet, bean paste turnovers that you would find in the big cities are missing at Mimi's. If you must have dessert, go for the *Chocolate Cloud Cake* or one of the five housemade ice creams.

It's nice to know that dreams *can* come true.

The Galisteo Inn

9 La Vega (Off Highway 41), Galisteo. 466-4000.

Dinner:	6 P.M.-8:30 P.M. Wed.-Sun.
Features:	Full bar. Smoke-free. Smoking permitted on patio. Free parking lot. [Historical]
Price:	Expensive. Visa/MasterCard. Prix fixe dinners: $32.
Cuisine:	Eclectic Southwest.

*M*emories of a lazy, spring afternoon of readying your car and heading out for country roads can bring swells of pleasure to even the most jaded soul. Why not renew those pleasurable memories and quiet moments by making a day trip to The Galisteo Inn? And don't forget to call ahead and make dinner reservations.

The Inn, a 240-year-old hacienda, offers charming accommodations (think about staying the weekend), homey fireplaces, plenty of books, a dining room that begs for intimacy and romance, and creative food that will definitely fulfill any inn fantasies you may have been harboring.

Once you settle in for dinner, the prix fixe menu that changes weekly might offer the following: In the appetizer category there's *Tortilla Soup* with baked tortilla strips, queso asadero, and fresh cilantro; or *Spinach Salad* with roasted corn, poblano rajas, and Feta cheese.

Entrees like *Grilled Ruby Trout* with lump crab, cilantro pesto, and wild rice griddle cakes; or *Pork Medallions* with fresh nectarine salsa, fried sweet potatoes, and green beans; or *Sweet Potato, Onion, and Mushroom Ravioli* with a charred tomato-sage sauce; or *Venison Ragout* with wild mushrooms, creme fraiche and potato pancakes could be one of the evening's choices.

Dessert, included in the prix fixe dinner, range from *Sour Cream Green Apple Pie* with cinnamon whipped cream to *Wild Maine Blueberry Sorbet* with fresh raspberries and a lemon cookie to *Pecan Flan* with a red chile caramel sauce.

Over coffee, when conversation has lulled to a whisper, suggest to the lucky one who is with you to stroll the grounds before you blissfully retire to one of the rooms you intelligently had the foresight to book for the night. Sweet dreams. . .

Harry's Roadhouse

Old Las Vegas Highway. 989-4629.

Breakfast:	7 A.M.-11 A.M. Tues.-Sat.; 7 A.M.-1 P.M. Sun.
Lunch:	11 A.M.-5:30 P.M. Tues.-Fri.; 12 P.M.-5:30 P.M. Sat.; 1 P.M.-5:30 P.M. Sun.
Dinner:	5:30 P.M.-9:30 P.M. Tues.-Sun. Closed Monday.
Features:	No alcohol. Smoke-free. Smoking permitted on the patio. Free parking lot.
Price:	Budget/Inexpensive. Visa/MasterCard.
Cuisine:	American.

After Mr. Ford introduced us to the automobile, roadhouses began popping up outside city limits in America at a steady and rapid rate. Alcohol could be sold and served legally when it was not legal to sell it within the bordering town. Also, townsfolk wanted a more secretive, out-of-the-way place to indulge their vices and the roadhouse provided just that. Cars could transport them from home hum-drum to roadhouse fun in a matter of minutes, not hours. Another reason: Americans were passionately on the move to explore their country—vacations, road trips, Sunday outings—freedom at its best. Over the years, it was inevitable that roadhouses would take a different bent, evolving into destinations where first-class citizens could now bring along families for some good eatin'—homestyle food with beer and wine, maybe music. Which brings us to Harry's Roadhouse.

The highway Harry's stands beside was the main highway to get from Santa Fe to Las Vegas—thus, the *Old* Las Vegas Highway. Harry's used to be a gas station, then a gas station-cafe, and then The Nifty Cafe. And, now, through the TLC of Harry Shapiro and Peyton Young, this spot has been transformed into their own particular version of a roadhouse, with a slightly funky attitude that endures in New Mexico.

You almost need a four-wheel drive to get into the parking lot. But once there, an inviting pale blue door with a lavender border and a row of newspaper boxes greet you at the entrance. Inside the tiny foyer hangs a community bulletin board with notices, services, business cards, and spiritual messages.

Harry's consists of three rooms: a small front room with a counter and six stools faces the kitchen with four tables lined up in front of windows that look out onto the highway; the main interior dining room has gaily painted table tops and a long community table for sharing or large parties; and finally the patio, which is one of the best reasons to eat here in good weather. There are three over-a-hundred-year-old pine trees that flank the fenced-in, terraced, flagstone patio where tables are spaciously set apart under the trees, or beneath striped and checkered umbrellas to protect you from the New Mexican sun. The best table is under the pine tree on the upper left side of the patio.

In the summer, lots of sunflowers, hollyhocks, silverlace, mint, and sage share space with a charming stream that winds through the area to give a cool, calming atmosphere. Weber barbeque grills are fired up around 3 P.M. to start smoking up pork ribs, or grilled chicken for the dinner menu.

Quesadillas, a good *Burger* with fries, *Cajun Style Blackened Catfish* with grits, a *Grilled Tempeh Burger, Caesar Salad, Burrito,* and *Turkey Meatloaf* with mashed spuds round out the dinner menu. There are a lot of sandwiches to choose from at lunch: *Catfish Po'Boy* with jalapeño tartar sauce, *Grilled Chicken Breast* with spicy BBQ sauce and *Smoked Gouda* on a bun, *Grilled Eggplant* with goat cheese, black olive paste and grilled tomatoes, and a *Turkey Reuben.*

All the pies are made on the premises and include one of my favorites, *Coconut Cream Pie.* There's also apple and pecan and a chocolate layer cake.

And, of course, there's the "almost famous" homemade ice cream sandwiches that carry a lot of weight with the locals as being so.

Early morning hours offer hearty breakfasts: eggs, home fries, a burrito with a filling of bacon, eggs, and potatoes topped with red or green chile and melted cheese, Huevos Rancheros, bagels with cream cheese, oatmeal, scrapple, pancakes, a whole wheat waffle with spiced apples and cinnamon butter, and, last, but not least, granola with fresh fruit and yogurt.

Don't be surprised if you see a lot of tie-dye T-shirts here side-by-side with cowboy boots, Stetsons, and yuppie linen. With Bob Dylan singing in the background and a bottle of Melinda's "World's Hottest" original habanero pepper sauce on every table along with Grey Poupon, you'll know this roadhouse has turned into a special New Mexican eatery where locals, travelers, and, yes, commuters love to come.

San Marcos Enterprises Feed Store & Cafe

Rt. 2, Box 150, Highway 14 South. (Highways 14 & 22). 471-9298.

Breakfast/Lunch:	8 A.M.-2 P.M. daily.
Dinner:	5:30 P.M.-8 P.M. Fri. & Sat.
Features:	No alcohol.1 Smoke-free. Free parking lot.
Price:	Budget/Inexpensive. Visa/MasterCard.
Cuisine:	American.

*K*ids love this place—ages five to ninety-five. Chickens, ducks, and geese roam freely around the cafe and feed store in the back. I always visit just to see the roaming fowl, and check out feed store items that I would never see otherwise.

On weekends there's usually an old-timey fiddle or banjo being played (sometimes too loudly) but the music adds to the country setting.

It's just plain fun to journey out this far from town, take in a bit of history, and explore the Turquoise Trail. The food here is simple and ample. There are quiches, egg dishes (fresh eggs from all those chickens), nachos, cinnamon rolls, green and red chile stews, sandwiches, burgers, and, unexpectedly, *German Goulash*.

Desserts tend to be the carrot cake variety although the *Apple Pie with Bourbon Sauce* isn't bad.

After lunch keep truckin' on to Madrid to do a little shopping at Maya Jones Imports for the best Guatamala has to offer. Say "hi" to owner Anne Kalminson (my favorite son-in-law's sister) and get the real lowdown on this old mining town.

Atalaya
See Restaurant listing on page 88

Cloud Cliff Bakery-Cafe & Artspace
See Restaurant Listing on page 117

Fano Bread Company

4605 McCloud Avenue, Albuquerque. 884-5555.

Hours: 8 A.M.-10 P.M. Sun.-Fri. Closed Saturday.

*F*ano Bread Company created a buzz when their *Rustic Loaf* first began appearing at Kaune's on Old Santa Fe Trail. It became so popular with Santa Feans that it was sold out every day before the store could close its doors.

Now you can find their Rustic Loaf in most markets and in some of the finer restaurants in Santa Fe such as Poulet Patate and Bistro 315. Since they first took the town by storm, new additions have appeared, like their *Sourdough Olive Loaf, Baguettes,* and *Levin.*

What makes it so in demand? Thick, crisp crust outside and light, chewy insides—just like the kind of bread that is favored in many parts of Europe.

The French Pastry Shop
See Restaurant Listing on page 44

Pásale Bakery
See Restaurant Listing on page 94

Plaza Bakery-Haagen Daz
See Restaurant listing on page 46

Sage Bakehouse

535 Cerrillos Road, Suite C. 820-7243.

Hours: 7 A.M.-7 P.M. Mon.-Fri.; 8:30 a.m.-5 P.M. Sat.; 9 A.M.-1 P.M. Sun.

*O*wner, Andree Falls, put together, on site, 3000 pieces of a special French oven that was shipped from France to Santa Fe. This particular type of oven turns out what is called "hearth-baked" breads. The bread-making process (all the dough is hand-scaled and hand-formed) takes twelve to fifteen hours from start to finish. Only one loaf, the *Pane Paisano,* incorporates a tiny bit of yeast. All the other loaves are yeast-free and use a natural starter method.

Crunchy caramel crusts, chewy, light interiors, intense flavors, and fresh-daily loaves are the end result of so much care and attention to details in this European-style bakery. The *Kalamata Olive* loaf is superb (at last, an olive loaf with taste and distinction) and the *Cinnamon Raisin* farm-based bread laced with cinnamon, raisins, and honey will hook you for good.

All Sage's breads are bagged in handsome paper packaging to ensure the natural transfer of air and moisture that is extremely important to maintain the bread's crust and interior.

There's yummy sandwiches made in-house on Sage's *Pane Paisano* to go with your espresso or juice. And you can sit either inside or out.

Wild Oats
See Market Listing on page 160

Zia Bakery
See Restaurant listing on page 99

Elizabeth's Gallina Canyon Farm

Box 706, Abiquiu, NM. 87510. 685-4888.
Fifty miles North of Santa Fe in the Chama River Valley.
Tour & lecture hours: 12:30 P.M. Tues., Thurs., Fri. (Summer only.)

*T*his grand lady of farming (and possible incarnation of Mother Earth) demands a heading of her own, and rightly so.

Way back when, Elizabeth Berry purchased remote and rugged wilderness land in the same vicinity as Christ in the Desert Monastary and dubbed it the "Ranch." Thus began what is now considered a farming legend.

Because the journey to the Ranch is lengthy, albeit breathtakingly beautiful, Berry decided to relocate most of her commercial produce farming and extensive gardens to a newer and closer-to-town chunk of land in the Chama River Valley, near Abiquiu—Elizabeth's Gallina Canyon Farm. Here, her working gardens are opened in the summertime to visitors for lunchtime talks, tours, and garden-growing philosophy. And, if you're so inclined, you can visit Elizabeth's adaptation of Georgia O'Keeffe's vegetable garden from the late 1940s.

Berry's diligent development of heirloom beans has sparked a national, if not international, interest in the restaurant industry. These beautiful, near-to-extinction beans were the kind our Grandmothers and Great-grandmothers used to grow in their gardens to nourish a nation. Now, with Berry's green-thumb determination, many of the heirloom beans grown at Gallina Canyon Farm are sold to chefs and their restaurants with amazing success—in Santa Fe and around the world. (Better Santa Fe restaurants like Cafe Escalera and Andiamo! have hosted heirloom bean tastings for chefs and food critics in Santa Fe, offering up to thirty different types of gorgeous beans. The tastings play an important role in the growing process—the most desirable beans are grown in greater quantity for a bigger market.)

In addition to the beans, the Farm grows mostly organic herbs, vegetables, and salad greens (her arugula and baby squash blossoms are the finest I've ever had) that appear every summer at Santa Fe's Farmer's Market and on the tables of the city's finest restaurants.

The Ranch remains a personal haven for Elizabeth Berry. Fortunate friends (many of them chefs) of Berry's are often invited out to the Ranch for a day of cooking, feasting, and gardening. There is no electricity here. But luckily, there is a generator that gets turned on for three purposes: music, vacuuming the main house *or* running the electric ice cream churn for the party of the day—period.

God bless Elizabeth Berry.

The Santa Fe Wine & Chile Fiesta

**Hilton Hotel of Santa Fe. 100 Sandoval Street.
Information: 1-800-336-3676.**

*T*he Santa Fe Wine & Chile Fiesta kicks off in late September, just in time for New Mexico's legendary chile harvest. The ever-expanding four-day Fiesta has grown to include a series of food and wine seminars with the likes of Diane Kennedy, author of *The Art of Mexican Cooking;* cooking demonstrations with Deborah Madison, author of *The Greens' Cookbook* and *The Savory Way;* tours to Chimayó, Georgia O'Keeffe's home, and Elizabeth Berry's Abiquiu farm; a Champagne and Dirty Boots Barbeque Brunch; over twenty-four winemaker dinners at thirty Santa Fe restaurants; The Gruet at Cochiti Lake Golf Classic featuring Gruet Winery's fine wines paired with food from Santa Fe restaurants every third hole; and the Big Bottle Auction wine auction. Most of the festivities build up to the big-top-tent-event on Saturday, The Grand Food & Wine Tasting situated next to the Hilton Hotel.

The tasting event features more than 180 different wine vintages from more than sixty wineries around the world and pairs them with excellent food from sixty of Santa Fe's restaurants—featuring chile dishes, of course. The result is a day of shoulder-to-shoulder rubs with famous chefs, writers, restaurant owners, extraordinary wine-makers, and foodies who all get into the right frame of mind to pay homage to food and wine.

The trick, if you can do it, is to taste, not swallow, the wine and nibble at the fabulous food. I must confess that last year I swallowed most of the wine and ate a lot of the food resulting in a tipsy head and expanded tummy—and a bunch of fun.

Albertson's in DeVargas Center

199 Paseo de Peralta. 988-2804.

Hours: 6 A.M.-midnight daily.
Features: Alcohol. Major credit cards.

This always-crowded Northside supermarket delivers home-town service, a butchershop, and specialty items—especially in the produce department.

There are lots of products here that keep New Mexican cooking alive and well in the home kitchen. All this keeps Albertson's popular with died-in-the-wool foodies who can usually find what they want here. And, of course, it's a continual favorite for those who have been coming here for many years.

Alfalfa's

333 W. Cordova Road. 986-8667.

Hours: 7:30 A.M.-10 P.M. daily.
Features: No alcohol. MasterCard.

By now everyone knows that Alfalfa merged into the Wild Oats enterprise, but keeps a separate name identity. Organic vegetables reign supreme as well as a great selection of hormone-free meats. They pride themselves on their natural beef and pork, both with lower fat, and sausages and chickens.

Turkeys from Diestel Farms could be the best in the country. Their superior taste is a far cry from the water-injected commercial turkeys we've come to accept as the only type bird available for our tables. The Diestel Farms birds are so good you'll want to prepare them often, not just at Thanksgiving.

Most everything here is also at Wild Oats with slight differences. Shop at either one or the other and you'll feel 100 percent healthier for having done so.

Plus: a great place to stop in the wee hours of the morning for fine, fresh-brewed coffee, and one of the best cinnamon rolls in town.

Cookworks

---

316 S. Guadalupe Street. 988-7676.

Hours: 10 A.M.-5:30 P.M. Mon.-Fri.; 9:30 A.M.-5:30 A.M. Sat.;
                 11 A.M.-5 P.M. Sun.
Features: No alcohol. Major credit cards.

*T*hree attractive buildings house three separate but same-owner stores, all clustered together on Guadalupe Street. The first store offers packaged gourmet foods and those hard-to-get specialty items like several brands of Italian Panetone at Christmas, syrups, salsas, coffees, teas, pancake mixes, and cocoas.

They sell coffee machines, tea pots, specialty magazines, plus Belgian chocolates from a glass case. There's also take-out that can be pricey, but worth it.

In the second building exquisite flatware, glasses, plates, linens and such, including some antique sterling serving pieces you'll drool over, can weaken even the sturdiest shopper's knees.

And last, the third store is one of the best cookware and cookbook stores in Santa Fe. Anything is here, from Le Cruset to Calphalon to tart rings to oversized wicker baskets to cookie molds to glassware to gadgets and knives.

Take time out to browse all three.

Coyote Cafe General Store

---

132 W. Water Street. 982-2454.

Hours: 10 A.M.-9 P.M. daily in summer. Check for winter hours.
Features: No alcohol. Major credit cards.

*S*o chock-full of packaged goodies, it's hard to turn around to see what's next on their over-stuffed shelves. Chile prevails with hundreds of salsas from all over the world (including my favorite, Coyote's own label, *Coyote Cocina Fire-Roasted Salsa*) that have a heat range from hotter-than-hell to heavenly mild. Lots of foodstuffs can keep you looking for hours: Piñon coffee beans, T-shirts, hats, cowboy mugs and plates, flapjack mixes, jams and jellies, baked-daily-chile-infused breads, candies, cactus edibles, chile posters, and cookbooks—with an emphasis on Mark Miller's publications, of course.

Edible

323 Aztec Street. 983-4699.

Take out:	10 A.M.-7 P.M. Tues.-Sat.
Features:	No alcohol. Catering.
Price:	Inexpensive/Moderate. No credit cards.

*E*dible's owners, Corey McGillicuddy and Keith McIntosh, have created a much needed take-out and catering business. There are lots of savory selections: *Crudites with Chipotle Aioli, Baked Cheddar-wrapped Olives, mini Country Biscuits with Smoked Turkey and Honey Mustard;* soups like *Chilled Red Pepper, Curried Carrot* or *Lobster Bisque;* fresh salads with in-season vegetables like sweet yellow beets; lots of pasta and rice choices, and side vegetable dishes.

Entrees might include their perfectly *Poached Whole Salmon* with cucumber yogurt sauce, *Chicken Breasts* stuffed with spinach and ricotta cheese, or *Black Bean and Calabicitas Tamales* with cilantro sauce.

Sweet selections could be *English Trifle, Queen of Sheba Chocolate Torte,* or a *Piñon Tart.*

All of their catering menu selections can be ordered two days in advance for your next dinner party, helping to make it effortless and delicious. Corey and Keith are happy to help you make up your menu as well.

Kaune Food Town

511 Old Santa Fe Trail. 982-2629.

Hours:	8:30 A.M.-6:50 P.M. Mon.-Sat.
Features:	No alcohol. Free parking lot. Major credit cards.

*T*his is Santa Fe's sweetheart-of-a-market, and deservedly so. Kaune's, pronounced Connie's (customers have added the plural), still has a real butcher counter in the back and it's bustling. The butchers are friendly and know what they're doing—custom orders are welcome. Most of their beef is U.S.D.A. Prime and they carry natural lamb, chicken, and meat. The term "natural" means the livestock is raised hormone-free. They even make their own carne adovada (take home and finish cooking). Sausages, Rocky's all natural, plump and great tasting chickens, hormone-free lamb raised in Northern New Mexico, slab bacon, Smithfield Hams, Canadian pumpernickle and rye breads the size of a mailbox (sliced to order), Boar's Head deli meats, and Kaune's own chicken liver pate satisfy the most discerning of Santa Fe palates.

Molinari Dry Italian Sausages are here. And so are cheeses—a plentiful assortment of Italian, French, Danish, English, Greek, and American. They have mascarpone and clotted cream, too. There are foreign and domestic selections of crackers, cookies, pastas, butters, olive oils, condiments, canned seafoods (the only place in Santa Fe I know where you can get the Julia Child-recommended salad niçoise ingredient, tuna packed in Italian olive oil), soups, sauces, spices, pancake mixes, cocoas, coffees (they carry *illy caffè*), teas, waters, and candies.

They also carry a fine assortment of oversized, hand-made candles. You'll find some local stuff in the freezers like the Pink Adobe's apple pies and green chile stew. The deli case offers lots more items made out-of-house by "Madeline" like a terrific egg salad and meat loaf to go. Rotisserie chickens (the seasoning is cooked right in) are in constant demand. The small produce section can be dissapointing but they do carry Vidalia onions in season. Some of the check-out folks have been here forever and are truly helpful and friendly.

The Marketplace

627 W. Alameda. 984-2852.

Hours: 7:30 A.M.-9 P.M. Mon.-Sat. 9 A.M.-8 P.M. Sun.
Features: No alcohol. Free parking lot. Visa/MasterCard.

This neighborhood market is the original natural food store in Santa Fe. Things got shakey when the giant markets moved into town but now everything's balancing out. Fine organic produce, a decent vitamin and mineral selection, daily take-out, salad bar, and good assortments of organic chips, cookies, condiments, dried fruits, canned goods, cereals, and juices, all make this small and convenient market good to stop in for picnic supplies.

Then stroll across the street and sit under a big tree by the Santa Fe River and go with the flow.

Ohori's

507 Old Santa Fe Trail. 988-7026.

Hours: 9 A.M.-6 P.M. **Mon.-Sat. Closed Sun.**
Features: **No alcohol. Free parking lot. Major credit cards.**

*O*hori's imports and roasts their own beans (dark roasts are the specialty). Primarily a take-out, you can have a cup of coffee or espresso and pastry to eat while you wait for your coffee order. (Complimentary cups of coffee are offered with your order.)

All the familiar sounding coffees of the world are here such as Aged Sumatra, Nicaragua, Kenya, Yemen Mocha, Tres Estrella, Costa Rica, French, and Vienna. Lots of exotic teas, chocolates, and cocoas are here with Italian ceramic plates and espresso cups to go with. Linen and damask dishtowels, tiny Japanese tea pots and cups, different styles of coffee machines, unusual tablecloths and napkins, books, cards, packaged candied ginger and violets, and lots of biscotti round out the commodities.

For convenience, you can mail order coffee beans, whole or ground to order, and any choice from a fine selection of teas.

Santa Fe Area Farmer's Market

Parking lot at Sanbusco Market Center off Montezuma. 983-4098.

Hours: 7 A.M.-11:30 P.M. **Tues & Sat.; 9 A.M.-1 P.M. Sun.**
              Opens mid-May through first Saturday in November.
Features: **Year-round inside market located in the Gross-Kelly Building next to Tomasita's in the Railyard. Special Christmas market inside Sanbusco Market Center, first two Sundays in December.**

*L*ocal bread and pie bakers, honey and jam makers, truckloads of wreaths and flowers, pick-up trucks full of fresh-picked sweet white corn and Fort Union melons, oils, cheeses, bushels of apples—all join forces to make up this necessary outlet for some of the best home-grown products and produce available during New Mexico's short growing season.

Buy bulging bags of organic, exotic greens, perfect yellow squash blossoms, baby yellow beets, and arugula from organic farmers like Elizabeth Berry, known far and wide for her green thumb and heirloom beans. Fresh-picked squashes and pumpkins are delivered in flat-bed trucks; there are garlics, onions, fingerling potatoes, and all kinds of herbs. (Each farmer has a sign out in front of their stall indicating organic produce.)

Get there early—the farmers are ready at 7 A.M.— because, like the Flea, the great stuff disappears fast!

Sunset Spirits and General Store

Old Las Vegas Highway. 982-6705.

Hours:	**7 A.M.-10 P.M. daily.**
Features:	**Beer/wine/liquor. Free parking lot. Major credit cards.**

A wacky-wonderful market that used to be a gas stop until owner, Allen Jung, from South Korea, took it over. Now it's like entering an oriental street market complete with sushi-bar (locals claim this could be the best sushi around), and Chinese take-out.

Mysterious Chinese herbal medicines abound and just about everything else. Walk to the room way in the back where you'll find an incredible selection of French and domestic wines, Italian wines, beers, and liquors. The wines are reasonably priced and the choices reveal a knowledgeable distributor. The wafting odors inside may put you off, but the wines are worth the visit.

Wild Oats

1090 S. St. Francis Drive. 983-5333.

Hours:	**7 A.M.-11 P.M. daily.**
Features:	**No alcohol. Smoke-free. Inside and outside seating. Free parking lot. Visa/MasterCard.**

*T*his natural food mega-store upstart came from Colorado, but what a blessing. It's more of a gourmet supermarket with dozens of varieties of breads, rolls, oils, juices, cereals, bulk flours, grains, nuts, dairy products, non-dairy products, cheeses, meats, vitamins, lotions, and kitchenwares. Produce, organic or no, can be dazzling.

The store is beautiful with blond, wooden plank-floors, wide aisles, attractive take-out counters, and glass displays that will make you want to buy something.

Wild Oats' salad bar is big and ultra-fresh—some of the veggies are organic. There are usually five salad dressings ranging from real blue cheese to *Healthy Heart*—made without oil or fat. The hot take-out counter features six different pizzas, whole or by the slice; tomatoey spaghetti sauce with turkey meatballs; warming bowls and containers of vegetarian chili; or meatloaf with sage gravy and garlic mashed potatoes.

The menu changes daily. Cold take-out has gorgeous pasta salads, Thai chicken, stuffed baked potatoes (to heat up there or at home), samosas, whole marinated beets, Moroccan carrots, olives, sandwiches made to order, BBQ tempeh, curries, and more.

There's even a dessert take-out and a superb juice bar, squeezed to order.

The owners have provided a pleasant cafe-style eating area inside if you want to eat here. There's also an outside patio with umbrellas. Tired or tense? Get the fifteen minute massage that's offered in the store every day and feel your worries float away.

Kaune Grocery Co.

208 Washington Avenue. 983-7378.

Hours: 9 A.M.-6:30 P.M. Mon.-Sat.
Features: Free parking lot. Major credit cards.

No relation to the other Kaune, this long-time local store has a full suppply of wines, beers, and liquors. Great price specials occur from time to time such as *Veuve Clicquot Ponsardin Brut* (Yellow Label Champagne) at $25.00 a bottle. Check their ads and stock up when the price is right.

Kelly Liquor

2885 Cerrillos Road. 473-9022.
109 N. Guadalupe Street. 983-9680.

Hours: 9 A.M.-8 P.M. Mon.-Sat. Closed Sundays.
Features: Free parking lot. Major credit cards.

Two locations now provides Santa Fe with wine, beer, and liquor take-outs convenient to both ends of town. Well-stocked stores carrying lots of fine and unusual tequilas, beers, Scotches, and vodkas, and they will special order domestic and French wines. Aperitifs, liqueurs, cognacs, foreign and domestic, are here— and they can order anything else you want.

Kokoman Fine Wines and Liquors

Highway 285 North at Pojoaque. 455-2219.

Hours:	10 A.M.-8 P.M. Mon.-Sat.; Noon-8 P.M. Sundays.
Wine tastings:	4 P.M.-7 P.M. every Saturday.
Santa Fe Location:	301 Garfield Street. 983-7770.
Features:	Free parking lot. Major credit cards.

*D*iscriminating folks drive from all over to browse and buy at this comprehensive, warehouse-of-a-store where treasures of French and domestic wines—undoubtedly the biggest selection in Northern New Mexico—are available. Expert advice and service are provided by owner Keith Obermaier and staff.

Partners, Robert Witcher and Shirley Pisacane, will operate the Circus Catering part of the new Santa Fe store (perhaps the best catering service in Santa Fe) and Jamie O'Neill brings the same expertise we've come to expect of Kokoman to the new location as bar and liquor manager. The three-story Santa Fe Kokoman provides dine-in and carry-out deli goodies, a wine bar, a climate-controlled wine cellar for their private stash and also cellar space that the public can lease to keep their wines safe and correctly stored until ready to cork.

We love you, Kokoman.

The Winery

Inside Sanbusco Center. 982-9463.

Hours:	10 A.M.-7 P.M. Mon.-Sat.; noon-5 P.M. Sun.
Wine tastings:	4:30 P.M.-6:30 P.M. Fri.
Features:	Free parking lot. Major credit cards.

*L*ocated inside the Sanbusco Market Center, this upscale winery keeps a goodly supply of wines properly stored on their sides in attractive wooden racks.

Fine cognacs, champagnes, and special liqueurs are here, also.

Wine tastings on Fridays are fun, as well as serious, and the service staff is helpful and knowledgeable about their wines. From a cart outside their door, you can get the best cigars in town to go with the vintage port you picked up from The Winery.

DISTRICT LOCATIONS

The Plaza and Downtown Area

The Anasazi Restaurant 23
The Bull Ring 26
Cafe Cassis 27
Cafe Escalera 29
Cafe Oasis 32
Cafe Pasqual's 33
Cafe Romana 36
Carlos' Gosp'l Cafe 37
Coyote Cafe 38
Coyote Cantina 40
Evangelo's Mediterranean Cafe 42
The French Pastry Shop 44
Galisteo News 45
Grant Corner Inn 45
Haagen-Daz Ice Cream Shoppe 46
Hotel St. Francis 47
India Palace 48
Josie's Casa de Comida 49
Julian's 50
La Casa Sena 52
La Plazuela and Bell-Tower Bar 54
The Old House 55
Osteria 57
The Palace 58
Paul's 59
Piñon Grill 60
Plaza Restaurant 61
Roque's Carnitas 61
San Francisco Street Bar and Grill 62
Santacafé 63
The Shed 66
The Staab House at La Posada 67
Tia Sophia's 68
Woolworth's (F. W. Woolworth) 70

Old Santa Fe Trail

Bistro 315 71
Guadalupe Cafe 72
Old Santa Fe Trail Bookstore & Bistro 73
The Pink Adobe 74
Upper Crust Pizza 77

Canyon Road & Area

Downtown Subscription News 78
El Farol 78
Geronimo 80
Tibet Cafe 82
Trixie's Cafe 84

South Guadalupe Street/Sanbusco Center

Andiamo! 86
Atalaya Restaurant & Bakery 88
Aztec StreetCafe 89
Corn Dance Cafe 90
Cowgirl Hall of Fame 91
The Double A 92
A Bar (at The Double A) 93
Pásale Bakery 94
Portare Via Italian Cafe 95
Pranzo Italian Grill 96
Tomasita's 98
Zia Diner 99

North Guadalupe Street Area

Bagelmania 100
Bert's Burger Bowl 101
Il Vicino 102
La Bell's 103
Noon Whistle 104
Pizza, Etc. 105
Poulet Patate Rotisserie 106
Vanessie of Santa Fe 108
Whistling Moon Cafe 110

St. Francis Drive Area

Dave's Not Here 113
La Choza 113
Masa Sushi 115
Tiny's Restaurant & Lounge 116

Second Street

Cloud Cliff Bakery-Cafe & Artspace 117

Cerrillos Road

Baja Tacos 118
Chicago Dog Express 118
Horseman's Haven Cafe 119
Old Mexico Grill 120
The Pantry 121
(Posa's) El Merendero 122
Tecolote Cafe 124
Tortilla Flats 125

Cordova Road

Maria's New Mexican Kitchen 126
Marisco's "La Playa" 128
Pyramid Cafe 130

St. Michael's Drive

Chow's 131
Felipe's Tacos 132
Green Onion Sports Pub and Restaurant 133
Mucho: The Gourmet Sandwich Shoppe 134

Rodeo Road

Castro's Comidas Nativas Restaurante 135

SURROUNDING AREAS

Tesuque

The Bishop's Lodge 136
Tesuque Village Market & Bakery 138

Chimayó

Leona's de Chimayó 139
Restaurante Rancho de Chimayó 140

North of Santa Fe

Embudo Station 142
Gabriel's 143

South of Santa Fe

Bobcat Bite 144
Dim Sum—Then Some 145
The Galisteo Inn 147
Harry's Road House 148
San Marcos Feed Store & Cafe 150

TYPES OF CUISINE

AMERICAN

The Anasazi Restaurant 23
Atalaya Restaurant & Bakery 88
Bagelmania 100
Bert's Burger Bowl 101
Bishop's Lodge 136
Bobcat Bite 144
The Bull Ring 26
Cafe Escalera 29
Cafe Oasis 32
Cafe Pasqual's 33
Carlos' Gosp'l Cafe 37
Chicago Dog Express 118
Cloud Cliff Bakery & Artspace 117
Cowgirl Hall of Fame 91
The Double A 92
Embudo Station 142
The Galisteo Inn 147
Green Onion Sports Pub & Restaurant 133
Harry's Road House 148

Mucho: The Gourmet Sandwich Shoppe 134
Noon Whistle 104
The Pantry 121
Paul's 59
Pásale Bakery 94
The Pink Adobe 74
Piñon Grill (Hilton Hotel) 60
Plaza Restaurant 161
San Francisco Street Bar and Grill 62
San Marcos Feed Store & Cafe 150
Santacafé 63
The Staab House at La Posada 67
Tesuque Village Market 138
Trixie's Cafe 82
Vanessie of Santa Fe 108
Woolworth's 70
Zia Diner 99

BARBEQUE

Cowgirl Hall of Fame 91
Embudo Station 142

BREAKFAST & BRUNCH

Atalaya Restaurant & Bakery 88
Bagelmania 100
Bishop's Lodge 136
Cafe Pasqual's 33
Cloud Cliff Bakery & Artspace 117
The French Pastry Shop 44
Geronimo 80
Grant Corner Inn 45
Guadalupe Cafe 72
Haagen-Daz Ice Cream Shoppe 46
The Pantry 121
Tecolote Cafe 124
Tesuque Village Market 138
Tortilla Flats 125

CHINESE

Dim Sum — Then Some 145
Chow's 131

COFFEEHOUSES

Aztec Street Cafe 89
Downtown Subscription News 78
Galisteo News 45
Old Santa Fe Trail Bookstore & Bistro 73
Trixie's Cafe 82

EAST INDIAN

India Palace 48

FRENCH

Bistro 315 71
The French Pastry Shop 44
Poulet Patate Rotisserie 106

GREEK

Evangelo's Mediterranean Cafe 42
Plaza Restaurant 61
Pyramid Cafe 130

HAMBURGERS

The Anasazi Restaurant 23
Atalaya Restaurant & Bakery 88
Bert's Burger Bowl 101
Bobcat Bite 144
Dave's Not Here 113
Green Onion Sports Pub & Restaurant 133
Harry's Road House 148
San Francisco Street Bar & Grill 62
Whistling Moon Cafe 110
Zia Diner 99

ITALIAN/PIZZA

Andiamo! 86
Cafe Cassis 27
Cafe Romana 36
Il Vicino 102
Julian's 50
Osteria 57
The Palace 58
Pizza, Etc. 105
Portare Via 95
Pranzo Italian Grill 96
Upper Crust Pizza 77

JAPANESE

Masa Sushi 115
Sunset Spirits & General Store 160

JEWISH DELI

Bagelmania 100

MEDITERRANEAN

Cafe Escalera 29
Pyramid Cafe 130
Whistling Moon Cafe 110

MEXICAN

Baja Tacos 118
Cafe Pasqual's 33
Coyote Cantina 40
Felipe's Tacos 132
Marisco's "La Playa" 128
Old Mexico Grill 120
Roque's Carnitas 61

NATIVE AMERICAN

Corn Dance Cafe 90

NEW MEXICAN

Baja Tacos 118
Cafe Pasqual's 33
Castro's Comidas Nativas Restaurante 135
Dave's Not Here 113
Gabriel's 143
Green Onion Sports Pub & Restaurant 133
Guadalupe Cafe 72
Horseman's Haven 119
Josie's Casa de Comida 49
La Bell's 103
La Choza 113
La Plazuela 54
Leona's de Chimayó 139
Maria's New Mexican Kitchen 126
The Pantry 121
(Posa's) El Merendero 122
The Pink Adobe 74
Restaurante Rancho de Chimayó 140
The Shed 66
Tecolote Cafe 124
Tesuque Village Market 138
Tia Sophia's 68
Tiny's Restaurant & Lounge 116
Tomasita's 98
Tortilla Flats 125
Woolworth's (F.W. Woolworth) 70

SOUTHWESTERN

The Anasazi Restaurant 23
Coyote Cafe 38
The Galisteo Inn 147
Geronimo 80
La Casa Sena 52
The Old House 55

SPANISH/TAPAS

El Farol 78

TEA (AFTERNOON)

Galisteo News 45
Hotel St. Francis 47

TIBETAN

Tibet Cafe 82

BEST BAKERIES

Alfalfa's 155
Atalaya Restaurant & Bakery 88
Cloud Cliff Bakery & Artspace 117
Fano Bread Company 151
The French Pastry Shop 44
Pásale Bakery 94
Plaza Bakery (at Haagen-Daz) 46
Sage Bakehouse 152
Wild Oats 160
Zia Bakery 99

BEST FARM

Elizabeth's Gallina Canyon Farm 153

BEST FOOD EVENT

The Santa Fe Wine & Chile Fiesta 154

BEST MARKETS/TAKE-OUTS

Albertson's in DeVargas Center 155
Alfalfa's 155
Cookworks 156
Coyote Cafe General Store 156
Edible 157
Kaune Food Town 157
The Marketplace 158
Ohori's 159
Santa Fe Area Farmers' Market 159
Sunset Spirits & General Store 160
Wild Oats 160

BEST WINE/LIQUOR SHOPS

Kaune Grocery Co. 162
Kelly Liquor (two locations) 162
Kokoman Fine Wines & Liquors (two locations) 163
Sunset Spirits & General Store 160
The Winery 163